T0643246

HOW CAN WE HEI

Thank you for your interest in this product. **Irwin** *Professional* is the leading publisher of professional information for sophisticated consumers of business, investment, and financial institutions information.

From its inception in 1965, and through the acquisition of Probus Publishing Company, **Irwin** *Professional* has been known and respected worldwide for innovation, quality, and service in each of the key markets we serve. **Irwin** *Professional* is now positioned as the publisher of the largest and most diversified business and financial information product line in the book publishing industry. This position of strength and critical mass is vital in today's quickly evolving world of information delivery.

We have the information you need and can provide it in the format you require. To learn more about other **Irwin** *Professional* publications and to receive your copy of our complete products catalog, please take a moment to complete this form and return it to the **Irwin** *Professional* Customer Service Department.

Four easy ways to return this information:
- **Call** our Customer Service Department: toll-free 1-800-634-3966 extension 1956.
- **E-Mail:** ipro@irwin.com
- **Fax** toll-free: 1-800-926-9495
- **Mail** to Irwin *Professional* Customer Service, 1333 Burr Ridge Parkway, Burr Ridge, IL 60521

Be sure to include code **1956** with your request for additional information.

IRWIN
Professional Publishing®
code 1956

Name _____ Title _____

Organization _____ Address _____

Department/Floor/Suite _____

City _____ State _____ Zip _____

Telephone ( ) _____ FAX ( ) _____ E-mail _____

Did you purchase this book in a bookstore? Yes___ No___ If yes, please indicate the store/ location._____

What is the name and location of the bookstore where you primarily purchase professional reading materials?

_____

Please indicate with a ✔ your areas of interest:

- ❏ Operations
- ❏ Compliance
- ❏ Fraud and Security
- ❏ Retail Banking

- ❏ Investment Management
- ❏ Executive Management
- ❏ Human Resources
- ❏ Treasury/Risk Management

- ❏ Trust Services
- ❏ Lending
- ❏ Finance and Accounting
- ❏ Other _____

Please send:
- ❏ the Irwin *Professional* Bank publication and products catalog
- ❏ my complementary issue of The Irwin *Professional* COMMUNITY BANKER

BUSINESS REPLY MAIL
FIRST CLASS   PERMIT NO. 204   OAKBROOK, IL

POSTAGE WILL BE PAID BY ADDRESSEE

IRWIN
Professional Publishing®
ATTN: PEGGY CONDON
1333 BURR RIDGE, PKWY.
BURR RIDGE, IL 60521-0081

THE NEW CRA

THE NEW CRA
A Practical Guide to Compliance

FRANCIS X. GRADY

IRWIN
Professional Publishing®
Chicago • London • Singapore

This publication is designed to provide accurate and
authoritative information in regard to the subject matter
covered. It is sold with the understanding that neither the
author nor the publisher is engaged in rendering legal, accounting,
or other professional service. If legal advice or other expert
assistance is required, the services of a competent professional
person should be sought.

*From a Declaration of Principles jointly adopted by a Committee
of the American Bar Association and a Committee of Publishers.*

▼▼ **Times Mirror**
M Higher Education Group

Library of Congress Cataloging-in-Publication Data

Grady, Francis X.
    The new CRA : what bankers need to know / by Francis X. Grady.
        p.   cm.
    Includes index.
    ISBN 0-7863-1113-4
    1. Bank loans—United States.   2. Community development—United
States.   3. Discrimination in mortgage loans—United States.
4. Bank loans—Law and legislation—United States.   5. Community
development—Law and legislation—United States.   6. Discrimination
in mortgage loans—United States.   I. Title
HG1642.U5G73   1997
332.1'753—dc20   96–31816

Printed in the United States of America
1 2 3 4 5 6 7 8 9 0 DO 3 2 1 0 9 8 7 6

*To my parents, John J. and Veronica
Grady, who sacrificed much to provide
an outstanding education for their children,*

*To my mother, the college English
major, for instilling sound grammar
and writing skills from a young age, and*

*To my wife, Donita M. Grady, who
encouraged the preparation of this
book, knowing full well the huge time
commitment authorship imposes.*

Francis X. Grady, the founder of Grady & Associates, Cleveland, Ohio, is recognized as a leading authority on CRA and fair lending compliance. Grady & Associates' legal practice concentrates on the representation of financial institutions and provides advice on the full range of issues encountered in the financial institutions industry. Mr. Grady combines both government and private practice experience, as an attorney with the Federal Deposit Insurance Corporation in Washington, D.C., and as an attorney in private practice in Washington, D.C., and in Cleveland. A frequent writer and lecturer on banking law compliance topics, Mr. Grady has served as a contributing author for eight years to a four-volume consumer credit treatise for which he has been responsible for, among other items, the CRA chapter. Mr. Grady received his B.S.F.S. from Georgetown University School of Foreign Service in 1980, a Certificate of Advanced European Studies from the College of Europe, Bruges, Belgium, in 1981, and a J.D. degree from the Ohio State University College of Law in 1984.

Founded by Mr. Grady to provide specialized, cost-effective counsel to community banks and thrifts across the country, Grady & Associates represents over 70 banks and thrifts in matters involving CRA compliance, fair lending, general regulatory and securities law compliance, securities offerings by financial institutions, shareholder relations, and merger and acquisition transactions, with a particular strength in branch purchase transactions.

PREFACE

This book is an easy-to-use publication designed to benefit all those involved in Community Reinvestment Act (CRA) compliance under the revised CRA regulations introduced by the bank and thrift regulatory agencies in 1995. The book is not an academic study of what CRA is or should be, but a practical "how to" guide on strategies and measures that bankers can follow to attain a satisfactory or outstanding CRA performance evaluation. The requirements of the revised CRA regulations now impact multiple areas of bank operations, including residential mortgage lending, commercial lending, consumer lending, the institution's investment portfolio, the deposit side of operations, the retail branch and ATM delivery system, and the person or department in charge of the charitable giving function. For all but residential mortgage lenders, CRA compliance is an unfamiliar and traditionally unknown area of responsibility. This book advises all personnel and areas of bank operations on strategies and measures that can be followed to obtain a satisfactory or outstanding CRA performance evaluation.

The previous CRA format rewarded process. Bankers, in an industry more astute at managing the paper flow than virtually any other, became masters at the process-oriented nature of the former CRA regime. Now CRA performance is all about actual loan production and loan distribution to borrowers and businesses of all income categories. As the banking industry learns to adjust to a new method of test taking, it is essential to consider guidance from an adviser structuring financial institution CRA compliance.

This author is called upon regularly to advise financial institutions on the practical "nuts and bolts" issues of compliance and how to achieve CRA compliance with a budget and resources of modest means. As a practitioner providing advice on CRA, I was acutely aware of the general absence in other publications of information regarding the CRA's practical application. To fill this void, and thereby enable bank and thrift managers to structure a

CRA process that responds to the vagueness of application that continues to characterize the CRA assessment process, I have provided insights on a number of everyday concerns, including: (1) how tough each of the four federal financial supervisory agencies is as a "CRA grader" in the CRA rating process (Chapter 9); (2) recommended documentation practices (Chapter 5 [the subsection, Performance Context] and Chapter 8); (3) the kind of loan distribution analysis that will satisfy both CRA and fair lending concerns (Chapter 5 [subsection, Performance Context] and Chapter 8); (4) avoiding violations of the CRA public file requirements (surprisingly the most frequently cited CRA violation under the old CRA enforcement regime); (5) conducting self-analysis of an institution's market share (Chapter 5 [Performance Context], Chapter 9, and Chapter 12); and (6) taking advantage of the process-oriented items that remain in the revised CRA evaluation regime (Chapter 5 [Performance Context], Chapter 5 [CRA Public File and Notice], and Appendix 2).

This book is written so that it can be read either on a chapter-by-chapter basis (generally corresponding to the subject matter indicated by chapter title) or cover-to-cover. Chapter 1 discusses the coverage and applicability of CRA, with a brief explanation of how a regulated financial institution's CRA obligations differ from the institution's fair lending obligations. For those who wish to understand how CRA has evolved into its present-day version, review of Chapter 2, Legislative History and Purpose of Community Reinvestment Act, is immensely valuable reading. Chapter 3 discusses the practical effect and the significance from an implementation perspective of the various transitional dates when specified CRA obligations apply to various types of financial institutions. Because definitions form the predicate for much of present-day CRA compliance, bankers should carefully read Chapter 4 (Regulatory Definitions).

Bankers should also read the appropriate subsections within Chapter 5 for the compliance requirements indicated for either a small or large bank. Chapter 5 offers many useful nuggets of practical advice (which are often in very short supply) concerning recommended documentation practices, review of an institution's market share, the quality and quantity of optimal loan distribution analysis, the kind of demographic information an institution must assemble to be on an even footing (or better) with its regulator, the role of the marketing function in loan production, the attainment of qualified investments, branch siting and exposure to charges of lending discrimination, the avoidance of public file violations (among the most frequently cited CRA violations under the old CRA enforcement regime and a likely continuing basis of violations under the revised CRA regulations), and favorably using the public file comment letter as one of the few remaining process-oriented opportunities in the revised CRA evaluation regime. Because the strategic plan option and assessment as a limited purpose or wholesale bank are so unique, those topics have been addressed in separate chapters (Chapters 6 and 7, respectively).

Chapter 8 (Documentation) is must reading for all loan officers and CRA compliance officers. While it is true the federal financial supervisory agencies no longer will consider detailed documentation of every contact or credit ascertainment effort to demonstrate performance, the effect of the revised CRA regulations for other than institutions evaluated under the small bank performance standards represents a considerable expansion of documentation requirements. Only the kind of documentation necessary to show CRA compliance efforts (but not the amount) has changed considerably under the revised CRA regulations. In other words, an institution should not throw away the shovel used to feed paper to the beast that lives within the institution's CRA files. Something has to feed that beast's appetite, and if it isn't paper—it could be the unsuspecting bank or thrift institution.

For those interested in the consequences of noncompliance, Chapters 9, 10, and 11 address ratings, the applications process, and administrative enforcement, respectively. For those involved in the "deal process" of banking expansion (for example, investment bankers, transactional attorneys, and executive management), Chapters 9, 10, and 11 may be the only chapters of interest for a reader with that perspective.

Finally, Chapter 12 anticipates the greatest effects of the revised CRA regulatory assessment process. A trend visible on the horizon in mid-1996 may foreshadow the greatest effect of the revised regulatory assessment process: A rising delinquency level for loans originated pursuant to nontraditional lending programs rekindles the debate whether community reinvestment activities are consistent with safe and sound banking practices. When the next cycle of credit losses occurs and the Treasury Department's full faith and credit guarantee of the FDIC deposit insurance funds is placed at risk, the 1990s' liberalization of loan underwriting practices may well recede.

ACKNOWLEDGMENTS

Richard D. Powers, Senior Vice President, Charter One Bank, F.S.B., Cleveland, Ohio, provided particularly insightful comments concerning loan production and loan distribution. Perry O. Adkins, Jr., the Director of Audit and Compliance Services at Capitol Federal Savings & Loan Association, Topeka, Kansas, one of the nation's largest remaining mutual thrift institutions, also provided helpful reviewer's comments.

Without the long hours and careful attention to detail of my secretary, Susan Timko, this book would not have been seen through to publication. She diligently typed and retyped multiple drafts of this manuscript during the several months this manuscript was in preparation.

Special thanks go to my wife, Donita M. Grady, who encouraged me to complete this book and tolerated my late-night arrivals and weekend writing sojourns at the office.

Francis X. Grady

TABLE OF CONTENTS

CHAPTER 1

Scope of Community Reinvestment Act

The purpose of the Community Reinvestment Act (CRA) is to require each federal financial supervisory agency to use its authority when examining financial institutions to "encourage" such institutions to help meet the credit needs of the local communities in which they are chartered consistent with the safe and sound operation of such institutions. The agencies encourage institutions to help meet the credit needs of their local communities in four ways. First, within the limits of the agencies' resources, their staffs provide information and technical assistance and will meet with representatives of industry and the management of individual institutions to explain the CRA, regulations, and examination procedures. This exchange of information helps institutions understand the purposes of the CRA and how the financial supervisory agencies implement the act. Second, as part of each CRA examination, financial supervisory agency staff may suggest ways in which the institution can improve its performance. Third, in decisions on applications, where CRA is a material factor, the agencies will publicly comment on an institution's record of performance. Fourth, the financial supervisory agencies believe that the availability of the public CRA performance evaluations serves as an additional encouragement for institutions to help meet local credit needs on an ongoing basis.

Financial institutions subject to the requirements of the CRA are institutions whose deposits are insured by the Federal Deposit Insurance Corporation (FDIC). The statute itself refers to these institutions as "regulated financial institutions." Therefore, credit unions, state nonmember banks that are not insured by the FDIC, and state-chartered savings and loan associations that are not insured by the FDIC are not subject to the CRA and the statute's affirmative duty to meet the credit needs of an institution's local community.

The scope of the CRA is limited further by the fact that the federal financial supervisory agencies are only to consider a regulated financial institution's CRA compliance record in connection with "applications for a deposit facility." The CRA statute defines this as an application for:

1. A charter for a national bank or federal savings and loan association.
2. FDIC deposit insurance in connection with a newly chartered bank, savings and loan association, or similar institution.
3. The establishment of a branch or other deposit facility by a regulated financial institution.
4. The relocation of any office of a regulated financial institution.
5. An acquisition of shares or assets of a regulated financial institution covered by the Bank Holding Company Act or the Home Owners' Loan Act of 1933 (the latter statute includes the Savings and Loan Holding Company Act).
6. Mergers, consolidations, or acquisitions requiring agency approval.

Specifically excluded from the definition of "applications for a deposit facility" are:

1. Applications for entry into the Federal Reserve System.
2. Branching and office relocations by state-chartered savings and loan associations.
3. Applications for deposit insurance by financial institutions that are not newly chartered.

Federal financial supervisory agencies assess an institution's lending record during regularly scheduled compliance examinations. Notwithstanding the anxiety the examination process induces in bankers, the CRA generally does not become a significant issue until a regulated financial institution makes an application for a deposit facility to a federal financial supervisory agency.

The CRA is only one factor of many that is to be taken into account in connection with the application. While the application of a financial institution with a poor CRA record can theoretically be approved, since 1989 the CRA enforcement environment has been such that institutions with unsatisfactory CRA performance routinely have had their applications denied. In March 1989, the four federal financial supervisory agencies—the Board of Governors of the Federal Reserve System (FRB), the Office of the Comptroller of the Currency (OCC), the Office of Thrift Supervision (OTS), and the FDIC—issued a joint policy statement (Statement of the Federal Supervisory Agencies Regarding the Community Reinvestment Act) regarding the requirements of the CRA and the policies and procedures the agencies will apply in evaluating a financial institution's CRA compliance and performance. The issuance of that policy statement marked a sea change in the CRA enforcement environment.

According to the *American Banker*, from the inception of the CRA in 1978 through 1988, regulatory agencies rejected only 8 of 50,000 applications because of substandard performance.[1] In February 1989, however, the agencies revised their approach to CRA compliance and since then have increasingly rejected applications because of substandard CRA performance. Table 1–1 shows the number of applications denied on the basis of poor CRA performance since 1989.[2]

While Table 1–1 shows that the number of applications denied on the basis of poor CRA performance has almost doubled over the last 6 years (15 denials compared to the 8 during the first 10 years of the CRA regulations), these statistics probably understate the case. Financial institutions considering expansion plans are aware of the role the CRA plays in the approval process. Many institutions table expansion plans in the event their most current CRA performance evaluation reflects an

TABLE 1-1

Applications and CRA-Related Denials by the
Regulators from 1989 through 1994

	FRB		FDIC	
Year	Applications	Denials	Applications	Denials
1989	761	1	2,056	0
1990	696	0	2,099	0
1991	551	1	1,839	0
1992	619	0	1,891	0
1993	821	2	2,181	0
1994	826	0	2,883	3
	OCC		OTS	
Year	Applications	Denials	Applications	Denials
1989	2,782	2	939	1
1990	3,149	2	893	0
1991	2,630	0	573	0
1992	2,610	4	837	0
1993	3,612	0	785	0
1994	4,368	0	1,010	0

Source: FRB, FDIC, OCC, and OTS.

unsatisfactory rating. Although there is no proof of it, it is virtually certain that the statistics concerning the number of applications denied on the basis of poor CRA performance are only the tip of the iceberg insofar as expansion proposals are limited by less than satisfactory performance. For expansion-minded financial institutions, CRA compliance typically receives the highest level of concern from executive management.

Many regulated financial institutions misunderstand the scope of their CRA obligations and their fair lending obligations. CRA, by the express terms of the statute, does not prohibit discrimination on the basis of race, sex, marital status, age, national origin, and familial status—the traditional prohibited bases of discrimination under the fair lending laws. The numerous consent decrees signed between lending institutions and the U.S. Department of Justice have as their principal focus the inquiry into a lender's obligation to refrain from disparate treatment, not an affirmative obligation to reach out to underserved groups. Special loan programs are developed to meet the credit needs of low- and moderate-income borrowers in response to the CRA, and one cannot deny the favorable impact such loan programs have on an institution's fair lending performance. But the last several years' tremendous investment of regulatory resources in rooting out lending discrimination affects CRA compliance secondarily. To the extent that a regulated financial institution engages in a pattern or practice of lending discrimination, violations of statutes which go to the fundamental basis of meeting community credit needs are significant adverse factors in an institution's CRA performance record. While numerous fair lending violations are very likely to subject the institution to a less than satisfactory or worse CRA performance evaluation, the converse proposition that satisfactory fair lending performance automatically equates to satisfactory CRA compliance is not axiomatic.

NOTES

1. See *American Banker*, March 18, 1989.
2. United States General Accounting Office Report, GAO/GGD-96-23, *Community Reinvestment Act: Challenges Remain to Successfully Implement CRA*, November 1995, p. 30, Table 1.6.

CHAPTER 2

Legislative History and Purpose of Community Reinvestment Act

[1] LEGISLATIVE HISTORY

CRA was intended to discourage redlining by financial institutions in areas perceived to have a high risk of loss where credit for home purchases or improvements is denied or restricted by onerous lending terms. Redlining, or geographic disinvestment, is a practice whereby lenders and insurers refuse to do business, or impose more restrictive terms for doing business, in an area of a community that is perceived to have a high risk of loss. Literally, redlining refers to the drawing of red lines on a map to indicate neighborhoods in which a lender would not provide credit.

In the 1960s, the problem of redlining became the focus of many political and social activist groups. Banks and savings and loan associations were specific targets of these groups because these institutions were soliciting and retaining deposits of the people living in redlined areas.

The Home Mortgage Disclosure Act (HMDA) was enacted in December 1975 to require financial institutions to compile data on residential mortgage loan activity. Congress believed that this system of data compilation would provide an early warning to neighborhoods of disinvestment activity by financial institutions. Congress also believed that the data could additionally be used as evidence to support claims of fair lending law violations.

The shift toward government involvement in the elimination of redlining practices was continued with the enactment of the Community Reinvestment Act of 1977 (CRA). The CRA requires federal financial supervisory agencies (a term defined by the CRA to include the OCC, the FDIC, the FRB, and the OTS), when examining financial institutions, to encourage the institutions to help meet the credit needs of the communities in which they are chartered, including low- and moderate-income areas, consistent with the safe and sound operation of these institutions.

Legislative history from the House of Representatives Conference Report reveals that the CRA had as its purpose the encouragement of "more coordinated efforts between private investment and federal grants and insurance in order to increase the viability of our urban communities."[1] From the time of CRA's enactment through the present, an area of conflict has been the relationship between community reinvestment activities and safe and sound banking practices. Senator Proxmire, the sponsor of the CRA, took the position that these considerations are compatible. He stated:

> The bill would not inject any significantly new element into the deposit facility application approval process already in place. Instead, it merely amplifies the "community needs" criteria already contained in existing law and regulation and provides a more explicit statutory statement of what constitutes "community needs" to make clear that it includes credit needs . . . [T]he bill is not intended to force financial institutions into making high risk loans that would jeopardize their safety . . . [T]here is no reason to assume that a high degree of community reinvestment is incompatible with bank safety. Rebuilding and revitalizing communities threatened by decline is good for the communities and good for banking."[2]

The principle contained in the CRA that institutions must serve the "convenience and needs" of the communities in which they are chartered to do business consistent with safe and sound operations is one that federal law governing deposit insurance, bank charters, and bank mergers embodied before CRA was enacted.[3] The Banking Act of 1935 declared that banks should serve the convenience and needs of their communities.

The Bank Holding Company Act, initially passed in 1956, requires the Board of Governors of the Federal Reserve System, in acting on acquisitions by banks and bank holding companies, to evaluate how well a bank meets the convenience and needs of its communities within the limits of safety and soundness. Under CRA, the concept of "convenience and needs" was refined to include extensions of credit.[4]

The statutory goal of increased community reinvestment is enforced in the current CRA statute through the twin levers of compliance examinations and application approvals. As seen from an economic perspective, the underlying premise of the CRA is that some sort of market breakdown exists under which qualified borrowers are willing to pay prevailing mortgage rates but are unable to secure a mortgage.

The CRA was amended in 1989 to provide that each regulated financial institution's examination rating and the regulator's written evaluation of each assessment factor be made publicly available. The same statutory amendment also established a four-part qualitative rating scale (Outstanding, Satisfactory, Needs to Improve, and Substantial Noncompliance) so that the publicly available CRA ratings would not be confused with the five-part numerical ratings (CAMEL 1–5) given to institutions by the regulators on the basis of the safety and soundness of operations. These safety and soundness ratings are confidential. In 1991, Congress further amended CRA to require public discussion of data underlying a regulator's assessment of an institution's CRA performance in the public CRA evaluation.

The Housing and Community Development Act of 1992 amended CRA to require that the regulators consider activities and investment involving minority- and women-owned financial institutions and low-income credit unions in assessing the CRA performance of institutions cooperating in these efforts. As amended by the Housing and Community Development Act of 1992, the CRA allows federal financial supervisory agencies to consider capital investment, loan participations, and other ventures undertaken by nonminority- and nonwomen-owned financial institutions and low-income credit unions that help meet the credit needs in the community where such minority- and women-owned institutions are chartered. Federal financial supervisory agencies may also consider certain transactions involving branch facilities of depository institutions that benefit minorities or women in determining whether a depository institution is helping to meet its community's credit needs. Specifically, in the case of any depository institution that donates, sells on favorable terms (as determined by the appropriate federal financial supervisory agency), or makes available on a rent-free basis any branch of such institution which is located in any predominantly minority neighborhood to any minority or women's depository institution, the amount of the contribution or the amount of the loss incurred in connection with such activity may be a factor in determining whether the depository institution is meeting the credit needs of the institution's community. "Minority depository institution" means one in which more than 50 percent of the ownership is held by one or more minority individuals and more than 50 percent of the net profit or loss accrues to minority individuals. Similarly, a "women's depository institution" is one in which more than 50 percent of the ownership is held by one or more women, more than 50 percent of the net profit or loss accrues to women, and a significant percentage of senior management positions are held by women.

The Riegle-Neal Interstate Banking and Branching Efficiency Act of 1994 amended CRA to require that institutions with interstate branching structures receive a separate rating and written evaluation for each state in which they have branches and a separate written evaluation of their performance within a multistate metropolitan area where they have branches in two or more states within the area. For institutions with operations in multiple states, the effect of this revision is that CRA performance is evaluated on a state-by-state basis. This makes it much more difficult for a financial institution to "hide" underperforming regions.

[2] HISTORY OF CRA REGULATIONS

Following the CRA's enactment in 1977, each of the federal financial supervisory agencies was assigned the responsibility of promulgating regulations to carry out the purposes of the

CRA. These agencies responded by jointly implementing regulations on October 12, 1978. Although the regulations were developed on an interagency basis and are virtually identical, each of the federal financial supervisory agencies has its own set of CRA regulations. For the Board of Governors of the Federal Reserve System, they can be found at 12 C.F.R. Part 228; for the Office of the Comptroller of the Currency at 12 C.F.R. Part 25; for the Federal Deposit Insurance Corporation at 12 C.F.R. Part 345; and for the Office of Thrift Supervision at 12 C.F.R. Part 563e. The requirements of the CRA are superimposed upon existing regulatory requirements relating to the convenience and needs test for chartering and branch approval.

Until 1995's dramatic and extensive rewrite of the CRA regulations, CRA performance evaluations focused on efforts by financial institutions to (1) ascertain the credit needs of the residents of their delineated CRA communities, (2) design and offer credit products that met those needs, (3) inform the public about the services offered, and (4) treat loan applicants fairly and in a nondiscriminatory manner.

Neither the CRA nor its implementing regulations contain an explicit prohibition of, or reference to, redlining. Congress and the supervisory agencies opted for an approach that encourages financial institutions to reinvest in certain areas, rather than set forth stringent guidelines or formulae for purposes of allocating credit. An original version of the CRA did contain provisions for credit allocation. As originally introduced, the CRA bill contained a section requiring the following:

1. Identification of a primary savings area from which the financial institution expected to draw half of its depositors.
2. Analysis of the methods by which the financial institution would meet the credit needs of its area.
3. An indication of the proportion of time deposit accounts of individuals of less than $100,000 obtained in the primary savings area that would be reinvested in that area.
4. A showing that the financial institution was meeting the credit needs of its community.[5]

These provisions were deleted before passage, and the CRA has not been viewed as requiring credit allocation.

Although by its terms the CRA does not require credit allocation, the increasingly frequent success of community activist groups in protesting applications can be seen as leading to "indirect" credit allocation. Since spring of 1989, many financial institutions, particularly money center and superregional banks, have voluntarily committed large sums to community investment.

From CRA's enactment in 1977 until March 1989, the CRA generally did not alone serve as a basis for rejecting an institution's expansion application. Since 1989, rejection of applications due to inadequate CRA ratings and the chilling effect such inadequate ratings have on untold expansion proposals are no longer uncommon. This is due to a number of factors, all of recent vintage.

Legislative initiatives, including the Financial Institutions Reform, Recovery, and Enforcement Act of 1989 (FIRREA), the Federal Deposit Insurance Corporation Improvement Act of 1991 (FDICIA), and amendments to the Home Mortgage Disclosure Act (HMDA), have had the effect of vastly increasing the amount and availability of information made public about institutions' CRA performance and lending records. Each of these changes represented by FIRREA, FDICIA, and the HMDA amendments has complemented the other, so that an institution's CRA evaluation is now made public, whereas it was not prior to July 1, 1990, and highly detailed lending information is made public pursuant to HMDA on an institution-by-institution basis. HMDA data inform interested parties' CRA analyses to an unparalleled degree, including the agencies' CRA analyses and those of interested community and consumer groups.

Following the foregoing changes, financial institutions have encountered a vastly increased degree of community and consumer group activism that is informed by HMDA data and institutions' publicly available CRA evaluations. The enhanced public profile of CRA issues and CRA performance has also gone hand in hand with the increased attention paid to CRA examinations and evaluations by the agencies in their consideration of applications.

The most casual observer of developments in the financial institutions industry could not help but take notice that, commencing prior to but gathering tremendous momentum in 1990, a definite trend has emerged whereby institutions involved in acquisitions have, both in connection with protested acquisition applications and in advance of the application process, entered into multimillion dollar lending commitments specifically addressed to lending and investment in low- and moderate-income areas. According to testimony presented on October 21, 1993, by Federal Reserve Board Governor Lawrence Lindsey before the Subcommittee on Consumer Credit and Insurance of the Committee on Banking, Finance, and Urban Affairs, U.S. House of Representatives, "the community groups who track lending agreements with institutions point to more than $30 billion in commitments for new credit."[6] The Fair Housing Act, the Equal Credit Opportunity Act, and analogous state laws have similarly served as bases for encouraging lenders to enter into such lending commitments.

This increased interest in CRA was accompanied by considerable criticism of the agencies' approach to CRA administration. The banking industry complained of too much emphasis on paperwork in a process-oriented evaluation system, and about the lack of clear standards. Small banks objected to the burden of compliance, and argued that CRA is unnecessary given the natural orientation of community banks. Community groups alleged that enforcement was weak, citing the few applications denied on CRA grounds and the fact that about 90 percent of institutions receive a "satisfactory" or better examination rating.

In July 1993, President Clinton asked the federal financial supervisory agencies to develop new CRA regulations and examination procedures to provide more objective, performance-based assessment standards that minimize the compliance burden while improving performance. In accordance with the President's request, the federal financial supervisory agencies held seven public hearings around the country and heard testimony from 250 witnesses, including bankers, community representatives, and state and local officials, about how CRA should be changed. As a result, the agencies went through two proposed rulemakings designed to implement the CRA in a manner consistent with the President's request.

As revised effective July 1, 1995, the CRA regulations provide more direct guidance to banks on the nature and extent of their CRA responsibilities and the means by which their obligations will be assessed and enforced. The revised CRA regulations seek to emphasize performance rather than process; provide greater predictability and promote consistency in examination; and reduce the compliance burden on some institutions. Specifically, the revised CRA regulations create a new system for assessing CRA performance, which (1) include measurements for lending, services, and investments; (2) require institutions other than small banks to collect additional data for small businesses, small farm, and certain consumer loans; (3) establish different evaluation standards and methods for small institutions to try to minimize regulatory burden; and (4) establish a new approach to assessment based on the financial institution's own strategic plan developed by the bank or thrift with input from the local community.

The revised CRA regulations promulgated in 1995 attempt to strike a balance between the concerns of community groups and financial institutions by focusing each agency's assessment efforts on three critical elements of lenders' efforts to serve low- and moderate-income communities and by establishing objective measures for assessing CRA compliance in the three areas: the extension of credit (the lending test), the provision of services (the service test), and the level of investment (the investment test). However, in line with the CRA's primary focus, the base element of the assessment would be the lending factor.

The revised regulations are substantially different from those that had been in effect since 1978. The revised regulations are intended to focus the assessment of CRA compliance on measures of performance rather than process. The revised regulations do not, however, tie specific levels of the objective measures to specific CRA performance ratings. Rather, an institution's CRA rating continues to be subjectively determined by examiners after a review of the institution's activities in light of the institution's capabilities and the needs of the community.

The revised CRA regulations reduce compliance burden as follows:

- Banks will no longer have to maintain extensive documentation demonstrating that directors have participated in formulating CRA policies and in reviewing bank CRA policies.
- Banks will no longer have to prepare a formal CRA statement, and a bank's board of directors will not have to review the CRA statement annually and note the review in the board's minutes.

NOTES

1. H. Conf. Rep. No. 95-634.
2. 123 Cong. Rec. S. 1202 (1977).
3. General Accounting Office Report GAO/GGD-96-23, *Community Reinvestment Act: Challenges Remain to Successfully Implement CRA,* November 1995, p. 18.
4. Id.
5. S. 406, Cong. Rec. S. 1202 (daily ed. January 24, 1977).
6. See 79 *Federal Reserve Bulletin* 1128 (1993).

CHAPTER 3

Timetable for Effective Dates of the New CRA Rules

The CRA regulation for each federal financial supervisory agency became effective July 1, 1995. On January 1, 1996, evaluations under the streamlined small bank procedures began. Institutions have the option to submit strategic plans for approval; data collection requirements are effective and institutions may elect to be evaluated under the lending, investment, service, and community development tests, if the necessary data is provided for the 12-month period preceding the examination. By January 1, 1997, institutions that will be subject to evaluation under the lending, service, investment, and community development tests must have identified their assessment area, although presumably delineation of the assessment area should have been made by January 1, 1996, as part of the design of appropriate data collection. By March 1, 1997, loan data collected for calendar year 1996 and the census tract listing within the assessment area must be reported. On July 1, 1997, evaluation under the lending, investment, service, and community development tests becomes mandatory, which also triggers a revised form of public notice lobby poster and the new public file requirements.

An institution that elects evaluation under the lending, investment, and service tests before July 1, 1997, must provide, in machine readable form, data on small business and small farm loans and community development loans for the 12-month period preceding the examination. The institution must also provide, in machine readable form, the location of home mortgage loans located outside metropolitan statistical areas in which the institution has an office (or outside any metropolitan statistical area) for that period. If the institution elects evaluation of any category of consumer loans, the institution must also provide consumer loan data, in machine readable form, for that category for that period. A bank or thrift institution that seeks evaluation under the community development test must apply for designation as a wholesale or limited purpose institution three months prior to the institution's examination and must provide data on community development loans for the 12 months prior to the examination. All institutions evaluated under the revised tests and standards or under any approved strategic plan before July 1, 1997, must delineate their assessment area in accordance with the provisions of the final rule.

In response to confusion about the transition rules contained in the new CRA regulation, the federal financial supervisory agencies, on December 20, 1995, issued an amendment clarifying that, when an institution either voluntarily or mandatorily becomes subject to the requirements of the performance tests and standards, the institution must comply with all aspects of the rule. Thus, once an institution comes under the new CRA regulations, the old version is no longer applicable.

Until July 1, 1997, there will be two sets of CRA regulations in effect. Generally speaking, only large retail institutions will be operating under the CRA regulations in effect for the first 18 years of the statute's existence. The former CRA regulations will be removed from the Code of Federal Regulations effective July 1, 1997. Effective July 1, 1997, large institutions will be subject to the lending, service, and investment tests of the revised CRA regulations, and wholesale or limited purpose institutions will generally be subject to evaluation under the community development test.

CHAPTER 4

Regulatory Definitions

With the introduction of a performance-based assessment process to replace the former process-oriented assessment of a financial institution's record of meeting community credit needs, understanding definitions established by the implementing regulation is crucial if an institution is to comply with the CRA. The CRA and implementing regulations assign specific meanings to terms used to assess an institution's record of meeting community credit needs. Because the CRA regulations are uniform among the various federal financial supervisory agencies, a financial institution should refer to the appropriate Code of Federal Regulations (CFR) cite to find the regulation applicable to it. For national banks regulated by the Office of the Comptroller of the Currency, the CRA regulations are found at 12 CFR Part 25. For state member banks regulated by the Federal Reserve Board, the CRA regulations are found at 12 CFR Part 228. For state nonmember banks regulated by the Federal Deposit Insurance Corporation, the CRA regulations are found at 12 CFR Part 345. For savings and loan associations and savings banks regulated by the Office of Thrift Supervision, the CRA regulations are found at 12 CFR Part 563e.

Because CRA performance evaluations under the revised CRA regulations will be based on much more specific criteria than the process-oriented CRA assessment of the previous CRA regulations, this chapter summarizes the most important definitions for purposes of the revised CRA regulations. Bank and thrift executives will discover that specific elements of CRA compliance have such specific meanings that every employee involved in the CRA process must have a clear understanding of those definitions which relate to responsibility for CRA compliance in his or her job scope or functional responsibility. Because the compliance requirements of the revised CRA regulations are predicated almost exclusively on behavior and actions that satisfy the regulatory definitions, an introduction to certain of the more key regulatory definitions is essential if one is to appreciate fully the compliance requirements described in the remaining chapters of this book.

Assessment area means a geographic area delineated in accordance with Section .41 of the CRA regulation. To simplify the process of delineating an assessment area, the revised assessment area requirement encourages institutions to establish assessment area boundaries that coincide with the boundaries of one or more metropolitan statistical areas (MSAs) or one or more contiguous political subdivisions, such as counties, cities, or towns. An institution is permitted, but is not required, to adjust the boundary of the institution's assessment area(s) so as to include only the portion of a political subdivision the institution reasonably can be expected to serve. This provision gives institutions some flexibility in their delineations, particularly in the case of an area that would be extremely large, of unusual configuration, or divided by significant geographic barriers. However, such adjustments may not arbitrarily exclude low- and moderate-income geographies from the institution's assessment area(s). For purposes of assessment area delineation, an institution should use the metropolitan statistical area(s) and consolidated metropolitan statistical area boundaries in effect on January 1 of the calendar year in which the institution is making the delineation.

The assessment area must include the geographies in which a bank or thrift institution has its main office, branches, deposit-taking ATMs, and the surrounding geographies in which the institution has originated or purchased a substantial portion of its loans (including home mortgage loans, small business and small farm loans, and any other loans the institution chooses). An institution's assessment area cannot extend substantially beyond a state boundary unless the assessment area is located in a multistate MSA. For institutions with branch operations in multiple states, there should be a separate assessment area for each state.

The requirements for delineating an assessment area are discussed in greater detail in Chapter 5[1].

Branch, as defined in Section .12(f) of the CRA regulation, means a staffed banking facility approved as a branch, whether shared or unshared, including, for example, a minibranch in a grocery store or a branch operated in conjunction with any other local business or nonprofit organization.

CMSA, as defined in Section .12(g) of the CRA regulation, means a consolidated metropolitan statistical area as defined by the Director of the Office of Management and Budget.

Community development, as defined in Section .12(h) of the CRA regulation, means affordable housing (including multifamily rental housing) for low- or moderate-income individuals; community service targeted to low- or moderate-income individuals; activities that promote economic development by financing businesses or farms that meet the size eligibility standards of 13 CFR 121.802 (a) (2) or have gross annual revenues of $1 million or less; or activities that revitalize or stabilize low- or moderate-income geographies. According to the supplemental information which appeared in the Federal Register for the final CRA rulemaking, the term does not require exclusive benefit to low- and moderate-income areas. This is an important distinction because low- and moderate-income individuals do not always live in low- and moderate-income areas. Thus, affordable housing for low- and moderate-income individuals in an affluent, upper-income suburb can receive favorable consideration as community development.

The converse, gentrification or lending to upper-income individuals in a low-income area undergoing urban revitalization, is not likely to be seen by federal financial supervisory agencies as activities that revitalize or stabilize low- or moderate-income geographies, although this is not to say that an institution should not characterize so-called gentrification lending as an example of community development. Lending to upper-income individuals in low-income areas undergoing gentrification would be favorably considered by regulators in their understanding of an institution's particular performance context and loan distribution analysis. Therefore, to the extent that institutions are engaged in lending to upper-income individuals who reside in low-income areas undergoing revitalization, the institution should be careful to articulate this in the description of the institution's performance context and loan distribution analysis. Because the definition of community development includes activities that revitalize low- or moderate-income geographies, an institution may be able to overcome the regulatory bias against considering gentrification lending as an example of community development.

Community development loan, as defined in Section .12(i) of the CRA regulation, means a loan that has as its primary purpose community development; and, except in the case of a wholesale or limited purpose institution, has not been reported or collected by the bank or an affiliate for consideration in the institution's assessment as a home mortgage, small business, small farm or consumer loan, unless it is a multifamily dwelling loan; and benefits the institution's assessment area(s) or broader statewide or regional area that includes the institution's assessment area(s). According to the supplemental information which appeared in the Federal Register for the final CRA rulemaking, examples of community development loans include, but are not limited to, loans to:

1. Borrowers for affordable housing rehabilitation and construction, including construction and permanent financing of multifamily rental property serving low- and moderate-income persons.

2. Not-for-profit organizations serving primarily low- and moderate-income housing or other community development needs.

3. Borrowers in support of community facilities in low- and moderate-income areas or that are targeted to low- and moderate-income individuals.

4. Financial intermediaries including, but not limited to, Community Development Financial Institutions

(CDFIs), Community Development Corporations (CDCs), minority- and women-owned financial institutions, and low-income or community development credit unions that primarily lend or facilitate lending in low- and moderate-income areas or to low- and moderate-income individuals in order to promote community development.

Other examples include loans to local, state, and tribal governments for community development activities and loans to finance environmental cleanup or redevelopment of an industrial site as part of an effort to revitalize the low- or moderate-income community in which the property is located.

There is considerable incentive for financial institutions to finance the environmental cleanup of so-called Brownfields (former manufacturing sites in central cities where redevelopment is stymied by environmental contamination and where the property is effectively abandoned). Given the significant liability financial institutions face when lending against environmentally contaminated property, only the largest financial institutions with full-time environmental specialist staff can be expected to navigate the treacherous shoals of this opportunity for community development lending.

Community development lending is politically favored and extremely beneficial in terms of garnering a favorable CRA evaluation for a bank or thrift institution. Accordingly, every loan officer should read and understand the definitions of "community development" and "community development loan." The reason that every loan officer should understand clearly what constitutes a "community development loan" is to make certain that an institution takes credit for the origination of community development loans and reports this to examiners during the examination process.

Community development service, as defined in Section .12(j) of the CRA regulation, means a service that has as its primary purpose community development; is related to the provision of financial services; and has not been considered in the evaluation of the institution's retail banking services under the service test performance criteria. Examples of community development services identified by the regulators in the supplemental information section of the CRA rulemaking include the following:

1. Providing technical expertise for not-for-profit, tribal, or government organizations serving low- and moderate-income housing needs or economic revitalization and development.
2. Lending executives to organizations facilitating affordable housing construction and rehabilitation or development of affordable housing.
3. Providing credit counseling, home buyer counseling, home maintenance counseling, and/or financial planning to promote community development and affordable housing.
4. Participating in school savings programs.
5. Other financial services, the primary purpose of which is community development, such as low-cost or free government check cashing.

Although neither the revised CRA regulations nor the CRA rulemaking so state, while a financial institution that offered free government check cashing to customers would receive some favorable evaluation for this activity as a community development service, considerably more favorable evaluation would be provided, consistent with the underlying philosophy and spirit of the term "community development," if the free government check cashing were also provided to noncustomers.

Voluntary activities in tutoring children, working with the handicapped or providing food to low-income people cannot be considered as a community development service because these activities are not related to the provision of financial services. A service must take advantage of an employee's technical or financial expertise to qualify.

For many, if not most, community banks and thrifts, the new definition of community development service represents a dramatic departure from activities that financial institutions characterized as having a "CRA tinge" under the previous CRA regulations. Yet as significant a change as the definition of community development service represents, community development service is also an activity that, with a little imagination and a minimum of investment, financial institutions can easily perform. Providing technical, legal, accounting, or MIS expertise to not-for-profit organizations and holding home buyer counseling seminars are common everyday aspects of many banks' business routine. Participating in school savings programs in elementary schools, as if a time warp from many decades ago, may make a strong comeback as an important element of community development service for many financial institutions. It merely requires some marketing imagination to appropriately package an institution's transaction account into a low-cost check cashing program that allows a minimum number of transactions with a low per-item charge. Lastly, many financial institutions provide free government check cashing.

Consumer loan, as defined in Section .12(k) of the CRA regulation, means a loan to one or more individuals for household, family, or other personal expenditures. A consumer loan does not include a home mortgage, small business, or small farm loan. The term includes a motor vehicle loan, which is a consumer loan extended for the purchase of and secured by a motor vehicle; credit card loan, which is a line of credit for household, family, or other personal expenditures that is accessed by a borrower's use of a "credit card"; home equity loan, which is a consumer loan secured by a residence of the borrower; other secured consumer loan; and other unsecured consumer loan. The five types of consumer loans permit evaluation of consumer loans on a product-by-product basis.

Geography, as defined in Section .12(l) of the CRA regulation, means a census tract or a block numbering area delineated by the U.S. Bureau of the Census in the most recent decennial census. Census tract is an area defined by the Census Bureau for the purpose of conducting an analysis of the population. The census tract will usually follow some sort of boundary, either a visible feature (such as a road) or an invisible feature, which is determined by the Census Bureau. Census tracts are found in areas that are or once were in Metropolitan Statistical Areas (MSAs). Block numbering areas are used in areas that do not have census tracts. A block numbering area (BNA) is an area assigned a number by the Census Bureau for the purpose of conducting a census or poll of the population, within a geographic area. BNAs are subdivisions of counties similar to census tracts generally used in rural areas.

A practical solution that many financial institutions will find attractive in obtaining block numbering areas, census tracts, and maps for an institution's service area is to contact one of the title insurance companies with whom a financial institution regularly transacts business. Many title insurance companies routinely have this information readily available and are pleased to share this information with their financial institution clients.

Home mortgage loan means a home improvement loan or a home purchase loan as defined in Section 203.2 of Regulation C (the implementing regulation for the Home Mortgage Disclosure Act, otherwise known as HMDA). Briefly, a home improvement loan, for the purpose of HMDA, means any loan that (1) is for the purpose, in whole or in part, of repairing, rehabilitating, remodeling, or improving a dwelling or the real property on which it is located; and (2) is classified by the financial institution as a home improvement loan. A home purchase loan, for purposes of HMDA, means any loan secured by and made for the purpose of purchasing a residential structure, including an individual condominium unit, a mobile home, or manufactured home. A home mortgage loan is located in the geography (the census tract) where the property to which the loan relates is located.

Income level is defined in Section .12(n) of the CRA regulation to include four income levels as follows: *low-income,* which means an individual income that is less than 50 percent of the area median income, or a median family income that is less than 50 percent, in the case of a geography; *moderate-income,* which means an individual income that is at least 50 and less than 80 percent of the area median income, or a median family income that is at least 50 and less than 80 percent, in the case of a geography; *middle-income,* which means an individual income that is at least 80 and less than 120 percent of the area median income, or a median family income that is at least 80 and less than 120 percent, in the case of a geography; and *upper-income,* which means an individual income that is 120 percent or more of the area median income, or a median family income that is 120 percent or more, in the case of a geography. For a bank or thrift institution operating in a non-MSA market, the institution should follow the statewide nonmetropolitan median family income to determine the appropriate income level.

Limited purpose bank or **limited purpose savings association,** according to Section .12(o) of the CRA regulation of each agency, refers to an institution that offers only a narrow product line (such as credit card or motor vehicle loans) to a regional or broader market and for which a designation as a limited purpose bank or thrift is in effect. A limited purpose institution may continue to be classified as such as long as it provides other types of loans on an infrequent basis. Depending on the type of activities in which the institution was engaged as of March 1, 1987, a so-called CEBA bank, a "nonbank bank" permitted under the Competitive Equality Banking Act of 1987 (12 U.S.C. §1843[f]), could be designated as a limited purpose bank.

Loan location, as defined by Section .12(p) of the CRA regulation, has different meanings depending on the loan type. A consumer loan is located in the geography where the borrower resides. A home mortgage loan is located in the geography where the property to which the loan relates is located. A small business or small farm loan is located in the geography where the main business facility or farm is located or where the loan proceeds otherwise will be applied, as indicated by the borrower. Thus, there may be occasions in which a bank or thrift may make a choice as to where a small business or small farm loan is deemed to be located for purposes of CRA reporting, if the proceeds will be used at a location other than the main business location. If the loan proceeds are to be employed in a low- to moderate-income area but the main business location of the small business or small farm is located in an area that is not a low- or moderate-income area, a lender is well advised to report the loan as having been made in the low- or moderate-income area in which the proceeds will be employed.

MSA, as defined in Section .12(r) of the CRA regulation, means a metropolitan statistical area or a primary metropolitan statistical area as defined by the Director of the Office of Management and Budget.

Qualified investment is defined by Section .12(s) of the CRA regulation to mean a lawful investment, deposit, membership share, or grant that has as its primary purpose community development. The following are examples of qualified investments:

1. In state and municipal obligations that specifically support affordable housing or other community development. Investments in municipal bonds designed primarily to finance community development generally are qualified and need not be housing related. Housing-related municipal bonds must primarily address affordable housing (including multifamily rental housing) in order to qualify. Investments in untargeted municipal bonds and standard mortgage-backed securities will not qualify. Investment in Federal Home Loan Bank stock does not qualify.

2. To support or develop facilities that promote community development in low- and moderate-income areas or for low- and moderate-income individuals, such as day-care facilities.

3. In projects eligible for low-income housing tax credits.

4. To not-for-profit organizations serving low- and moderate-income housing or other community development needs, such as home counseling, home maintenance counseling, credit counseling, and other financial services education.

5. In or to organize supporting activities essential to the capacity of low- and moderate-income individuals or areas to utilize credit or to sustain economic development.

These examples are the only qualified investments identified by the federal financial supervisory agencies during the 1995 CRA rulemaking.

Recognizing how restrictive the definition of qualified investment is, the regulators have begun to issue interpretive letters opining as to whether certain specialized investments satisfy the qualified investment criteria. An institution whose putative qualified investment has no ready match in the laundry list of recognized qualified investments is well advised to consider any written guidance promulgated by the staffs of the four federal financial supervisory agencies that supplements the CRA rulemaking process.

Small bank or **small savings association,** as defined in Section .12(t) of the CRA regulation, means an institution that, as of December 31 of the prior two calendar years, had total assets of less than $250 million and was independent or an affiliate of a holding company that, as of December 31 of either of the prior two calendar years, had total banking and thrift assets of less than $1 billion. When an institution exceeds the asset limit, the two-year period gives plenty of lead time to prepare to meet requirements applicable to large institutions. References to "small bank" throughout this book should also be understood to mean "small savings association" as the context may so require. In lieu of the term "savings association," the term "thrift" is frequently used throughout the book as a shorthand designation, even though the term "thrift" would by general industry practice include FDIC-regulated savings banks.

Small business loan is defined as a loan whose original amount is $1 million or less and that was reported as either "loans secured by nonfarm or nonresidential real estate" or "commercial and industrial loans" in Part II of a bank's Consolidated Report of Condition and Income (call report) or a savings association's Thrift Financial Report.

The revised CRA regulations permit financial institutions to receive favorable evaluation for small business and small farm lending. For many financial institutions, the inclusion of small business and small farm lending in CRA performance should permit commercial banks whose franchise lies in small commercial lending or ag lending to receive favorable CRA performance evaluation. The revised CRA regulations recognize that residential mortgage credit is not the sole basis of a healthy economy but that job creation in the small business sector of the American economy is equally important to the communities in which such small businesses operate.

Small farm loan means a loan included in "loans to small farms" as defined in the instructions for a bank's Consolidated Report of Condition and Income (call report) or a savings association's Thrift Financial Report. Small farm loans are defined as those whose original amounts are $500,000 or less *and* were reported as either "loans to finance agricultural production and other loans to farmers" or "loans secured by farmland" in Part I of the Call Report and Thrift Financial Report.

A loan to the "fishing industry" comes under the definition of a small farm loan by virtue of instructions for Part I of the Call Report and Schedule SB of the Thrift Financial Report, which include loans "made for the purpose of financing fisheries and forestries, including loans to commercial fisherman" as a component of the definition for "loans to finance agricultural production and other loans to farmers."

Wholesale bank or **wholesale savings association,** as defined by Section .12(w) of the CRA regulation for each agency, means an institution that is not in the business of extending home mortgage, small business, small farm, or consumer loans to retail customers, and for which a designation as a wholesale bank or savings association is in effect by the institution's principal federal banking agency. Depending on the type of activities in which the institution was engaged as of March 1, 1987, a so-called CEBA bank, a "nonbank bank" permitted under the Competitive Equality Banking Act of 1987 (12 U.S.C. §1843[f]), could be designated as a wholesale bank.

CHAPTER 5

Compliance Requirements

[1] DELINEATING ASSESSMENT AREA

Unlike under the CRA regulations in effect for the first 18 years following the statute's enactment, a federal financial supervisory agency no longer evaluates a bank's delineation of assessment area as a separate performance criterion, but the federal financial supervisory agency does review the delineation for compliance with the assessment area requirements of the rule.

The assessment area requirements of the regulation state that an institution shall not delineate an assessment area extending substantially across the boundaries of a consolidated metropolitan statistical area (CMSA). The assessment area must consist generally of one or more MSAs or one or more contiguous political subdivisions. The assessment area should include the geographies (each census tract or block numbering area) in which the bank or thrift has its main office, branches, or deposit-taking ATMs and the surrounding geographies in which the institution has originated or purchased a substantial portion of its loans (including home mortgage loans, small business, and small farm loans and any other loans the bank chooses). Including mobile branches and ATMs in defining an assessment area ensures that an institution that uses these means in an area not otherwise served by the institution will be evaluated on its success in helping to meet the credit needs of the area.

Out-of-area loan production offices and the area they serve need not comprise part of an institution's assessment area unless the bank or thrift has an approved branch office operating in that area. To illustrate the operation of this precept, consider the example of an institution with branch offices operating in the Cleveland, Ohio, CMSA and the Toledo, Ohio, CMSA. If that institution has a loan production office in the Indianapolis, Indiana, marketplace, the institution's assessment area need not include the Indianapolis CMSA.

If an institution serves a geographic area that extends substantially beyond a CMSA boundary, the institution must delineate separate assessment areas for the area inside and outside the CMSA and for different CMSAs. Moreover, the assessment area should not extend substantially across state boundaries unless the assessment area is located in a multistate metropolitan statistical area. For institutions with branch operations in multiple states, there should be a separate assessment area for each state.

Many managers considering the assessment area delineation have been uncertain about whether an institution's operations will qualify as those occurring in a multistate MSA. To determine whether an institution qualifies for this regulatory burden reduction, the institution should refer to guidance promulgated by the Office of Management and Budget concerning appropriate MSA-use definitions.[1] If the Bureau of the Census recognizes an MSA as a multistate MSA and the institution serves that geographic area, the institution can delineate a multistate MSA that crosses state boundaries without having to identify a separate assessment area for each state. Census information is available from regional offices of the Bureau of the Census as noted in Table 5–1.

To simplify the process of delineating an assessment area, the revised assessment area requirement encourages institutions to establish assessment area boundaries that coincide with the boundaries of one or more MSAs or one or more contiguous political subdivisions, such as counties, cities, or towns. An institution is permitted, but is not required, to adjust the boundary of its assessment area(s) so as to include only the portion of a political subdivision it reasonably can be expected to

T A B L E 5–1

Census Information

For census information, contact a regional office of the Bureau of the Census as indicated below. The list shows the states covered by each regional office.

Atlanta: (404) 730-3834
Alabama, Florida, Georgia

Boston: (617) 424-0513
Connecticut, Massachusetts, Maine, New Hampshire, New York (excluding New York City, and Nassau, Orange, Rockland, Suffolk and Westchester counties), Rhode Island, Vermont

Charlotte: (704) 344-6702
District of Columbia, Kentucky, North Carolina, South Carolina, Tennessee, Virginia

Chicago: (708) 562-1736
Illinois, Indiana, Wisconsin

Dallas: (214) 767-7482
Louisiana, Mississippi, Texas

Denver: (303) 969-7760
Arizona, Colorado, Nebraska, New Mexico, North Dakota, South Dakota, Utah, Wyoming

Detroit: (313) 259-3161
Michigan, Ohio, West Virginia

Kansas City: (913) 551-6750
Arkansas, Iowa, Kansas, Minnesota, Missouri, Oklahoma

Los Angeles: (818) 904-6339
California

New York: (212) 264-6272
New York (including only New York City, and Nassau, Orange, Rockland, Suffolk, and Westchester counties), Puerto Rico

Philadelphia: (215) 597-1189
Delaware, Maryland, New Jersey, Pennsylvania

Seattle: (206) 728-5557
Alaska, Hawaii, Idaho, Montana, Nevada, Oregon, Washington

To place an order for any census product, contact:
Customer Services Branch
Bureau of the Census
Washington, D.C. 20233
(301) 457-4100

serve. This provision gives institutions some flexibility in their delineations, particularly in the case of an area that would be extremely large, of unusual configuration, or divided by significant geographic barriers. However, such adjustments may not arbitrarily exclude low- and moderate-income geographies from the institution's assessment area(s).

Because the revised CRA regulations contemplate examiner assessment of lending performance on the basis of loan dispersion within the assessment area, many managements are fearful (and rightfully so) of delineating an entire county as an assessment area if the institution does not have thorough penetration of all geographies within the assessment area. Supplemental information which appeared in the final CRA rulemaking should provide some assurance to institutions on this score. If, for example, an institution delineated the entire county in which the institution is located as its assessment area but could have delineated its assessment area as only a portion of the county, the institution will not be penalized for lending in that portion of the county, so long as that portion does not reflect illegal discrimination or arbitrarily exclude low- or moderate-income geographies.

For purposes of assessment area delineation, an institution should use the MSA and CMSA boundaries in effect on January 1 of the calendar year in which the institution is making the delineation.

The assessment area(s) for a wholesale or limited purpose institution must generally consist of one or more metropolitan statistical areas or one or more contiguous political subdivisions in which the institution has its main office, branches, and deposit-taking ATMs. Because of how the assessment of the community development test is structured, an institution need not delineate a statewide or regional, rather than local, assessment area in order to receive consideration of community development activities that are outside an institution's assessment area, but that are in a broader state or region that includes the institution's assessment area.

Some financial institutions target a specific ethnic group in designing and marketing products and services. In an interagency interpretation promulgated by the Consumer Compliance

Task Force of the Federal Financial Institutions Examination Council (FFIEC), the agencies noted that an institution may direct the marketing of its products and services to one or more specific ethnic groups, provided that the institution can maintain compliance with the Fair Housing and Equal Credit Opportunity Acts (and this may not always be possible).[2] Institutions that target a single ethnic group, while having offices located in multiethnic areas, often exhibit significant lending disparities and unsatisfactory CRA performance. As a practical matter, therefore, unless the assessment area population corresponds to the targeted ethnic group, the designing and marketing of products and services to a specific ethnic group is likely to involve violations of the fair lending laws.

The federal financial supervisory agencies will use the assessment area delineated by the institution, unless they determine that the assessment area does not comply with the requirements for assessment areas set forth in the rule. If the assessment area fails to comply with the rule's requirements, examiners will designate an area that does comply and will use that area in evaluating the institution's performance. The revisions are to be discussed with the institution's management, and the revised assessment area is to be used by the examiners to evaluate the institution's performance. Unless the assessment area shows signs of illegal discrimination, the CRA examination procedures state that examiners are not to consider any problem with the institution's designated assessment area when assigning a rating to the institution. According to the examination procedures, any burden associated with an institution's delineation of communities and any inconsistencies resulting from examiners' criticizing community delineations as being too large at one examination and too small at the next examination should be eliminated.

Under the previous version of the CRA regulations, many institutions found themselves having to justify the basis for the institution's community delineation. The subjectivity of different examiners' perceptions, from exam to exam, caused substantial compliance work. The intended alleviation of this problem is one prominent example of regulatory burden reduction inherent in the revised CRA regulations.

The Riegle-Neal Interstate Banking and Branching Efficiency Act of 1994 amended the CRA to require performance evaluation on a state-by-state basis for institutions with operations in multiple states. This amendment responds to the criticism that a bank with operations in multiple states did not receive a CRA public performance evaluation that permitted the public to see how the financial institution was performing in different markets. That same criticism also applied to a financial institution with multiple markets in the same state. Although neither the CRA regulations nor the CRA examination procedures provide specific guidance concerning the aggregate CRA rating provided to an institution with operations in multiple states, a likely basis for evaluation would correspond to the percentage of total assets in the consolidated organization represented by a particular state or assessment area. The percentage of assets in each assessment area, both within a state and per state, is a likely basis for a performance evaluation when talking about institutions with operations in multiple states or multiple assessment areas per state. The market-by-market evaluation of a bank with multiple assessment areas should result in an overall rating that is a true weighted average of each individual assessment area.

This new performance evaluation method will permit the public to understand well those financial institutions which use one state franchise as a source to "mine" deposits and a different state franchise as the lending recipient of the "mined" deposits. This effect may explain why several of the large California thrifts have in the last several years divested themselves of the nontraditional portion of their franchises in the Midwest or East.

Although the CRA statute by its express terms requires a performance evaluation only on a state-by-state basis, third parties should be able to look through the performance evaluation for a particular state and assess performance within that state by understanding the percentage of assets represented by each assessment area within a particular state. Of course, from the perspective of community activists, requiring CRA public performance evaluations to likewise be provided on a market-by-market basis for the multiple assessment areas present within a particular state would represent the optimal public policy solution to the public's desire to know CRA performance in excruciating detail throughout an institution.

[2] PERFORMANCE CONTEXT

To take into account community characteristics and needs, the revised CRA regulations make explicit the performance context against which the tests and standards set out in the regulations are to be applied. This performance context includes consideration of six factors concerning the unique characteristics of the institution under examination and the market in which the institution operates. The appropriate federal financial supervisory agency will apply the performance tests (lending, service, and investment tests) and small bank performance standards, and make the decision to approve a proposed CRA strategic plan in the context of:

1. Demographic data on median income levels, distribution of household income, nature of housing stock, housing costs, and other relevant data.
2. Any information about lending, investment, and service opportunities in the institution's assessment area(s) maintained by the institution or obtained from community organizations, state, local and tribal governments, economic development agencies, or other sources.
3. The institution's products and business strategy, as determined from data provided by the institution.
4. Institutional capacity and constraints, including size and financial condition of the institution, economic climate, safety and soundness limitations, and other factors.
5. The institution's past performance and that of similar lenders.
6. The institution's public file.
7. Any other information considered relevant by the regulator.

An institution's federal financial supervisory agency will neither prepare a formal assessment of community credit needs nor evaluate an institution on its efforts to ascertain community credit needs. Instead, an institution's federal financial supervisory agency will request any information that the institution has developed on lending, investment, and service opportunities in its assessment area(s). The institution's federal financial supervisory agency will not expect more information than what the institution normally would develop to prepare a business plan or to identify potential markets and customers, including low- and moderate-income persons and geographies in the institution's assessment area(s). A business plan for CRA compliance is a standard not previously met by most community banks.

By gathering marketplace demographic information, a bank or thrift will be well positioned to shape examiner perceptions of the institution's performance context. The exercise of conducting a self-assessment before the arrival of examiners is good preparation. An institution would gather:

- Maps of census tracts and block numbering areas.
- Median income information for the MSA or statewide nonmetropolitan areas.
- Census information on income levels of various geographies, with stratification by the four income-level categories for the aggregate number of low-income geographies, moderate-income geographies, middle-income geographies, and upper-income geographies.
- General economic information for the institution's area.
- The nature of the housing stock (for example, owner occupied, one- to four-family dwellings, mobile homes, rental housing stock, number of building permits issued for single family residential and multifamily residential units).
- Average age and price of housing stock within given geographies.
- Employment data information identifying the number of business establishments within the assessment area, with a breakdown by the number of employees for

different employer staffing levels (1–49 employees, 50–499 employees, 500 or more employees).
- Employment data information by category of employer.
- Racial composition of the assessment area.
- Information, either formal or informal, about other local bank or thrift institutions, their product and service offerings, and their market penetration.

If the institution's community or strategies experience significant change, the information should be updated.

Concerning the assembling of information about other financial institutions, a financial institution should obtain, at a minimum, the public performance evaluations from competing financial institutions within that particular institution's marketplace. With this information and the other marketplace demographic information noted above, a financial institution should be well informed to articulate how the institution's product offerings and business strategy are consistent with the institution's performance context.

A considerable amount of marketplace demographic information is available from the U.S. Department of Commerce at the following telephone numbers: (301) 457-4100 for 1990 census data, housing, income, and population; and (703) 487-4778 for guidance on MSAs and CMSAs definitions. Such MSA information is available by writing to U.S. Department of Commerce, National Technical Information Service, Springfield, Virginia 22161. See note 1 at the end of the chapter.

Compiling the information necessary to develop a comprehensive understanding of an institution's performance context has spawned a cottage industry of providers offering programs, reports, data analysis, and so on. Recognizing the enormousness of the task, even the federal financial supervisory agencies themselves have outsourced to providers who do the necessary data gathering and analysis necessary for assessment under the revised CRA regulations. The April 25, 1996, *American Banker* reported that the OTS is using CRA Wiz, a data gathering and mapping product from PCI Services of Andover, Massachusetts. CRA Wiz permits the user to analyze a particular financial institution's lending patterns, as well as the lending patterns of the institution's competitors. The OCC, the sister federal financial supervisory agency to the OTS within the Department of the Treasury, is also using CRA Wiz. The FDIC relies on CRA Analyzer from Tactician Corporation for its data analysis, as do some Federal Reserve Banks. Many banks are discovering that mapping software from these and other vendors aids their CRA and fair lending compliance efforts and, more importantly, has revolutionized marketing choices.

Institutions will need to evaluate the market opportunities for each income level and the appropriate targeting of products and services. The CRA examination procedures for large retail institutions indicate that the examiner will gain a working knowledge of the institution's community by considering information provided from the institution along with information from community, government, civic, and other sources. The examination procedures note that information from community contacts can provide valuable insights for examiners, particularly those who have relatively little experience or familiarity with an institution's assessment area. The guidelines state that contacts may be made as part of an examination, or prior to the start of an examination, and typically will be made by those examiners responsible for the CRA examination. However, wherever possible, the examination procedures require examiners to draw on recent local interviews conducted by other agency staff members or by other regulatory agencies with CRA responsibilities.

An October 19, 1995, CRA teleconference conducted by the four federal financial supervisory agencies indicated that banking agencies will share knowledge concerning community contacts with regulated institutions. An institution should, in advance of any CRA examination, contact the federal financial supervisory agency to ascertain the list of community contacts maintained by that regulatory agency for that institution's market. Note that while the federal financial supervisory agencies claim an institution's CRA performance will not be based on outreach efforts to the community but rather solely on performance, many industry commentators believe the practical effect of insufficient outreach will be felt when an examiner interviews members of the community served by the institution. The new CRA regulations and examination guidelines notwithstanding, community outreach will still need to be a significant facet of any financial institution's strategy for attaining satisfactory CRA evaluations.

In a radical departure from past CRA compliance, business loans should be thought of as having CRA consequences. It is no longer appropriate to think of CRA lending and residential first mortgage and home improvement lending as one and the same—small business loans can have as much or more impact from a CRA perspective. This change is particularly favorable to banks significantly engaged in commercial lending to small businesses and farms. For the first time, a bank's efforts to make small business and small farm loans and the lender's underwriting practices will receive consideration under the lending test, and thus level the playing field with residential mortgage lenders insofar as favorable evaluation of lending performance. Management should therefore ascertain small business market characteristics.

One place to start compiling information on small business lending is a report prepared by the Small Business Administration entitled *Small Business Lending in the United States.* This is available from the Small Business Administration or from the National Technical Information Service, Springfield, Virginia 22161. See note 1 at the end of this chapter for more information. *Small Business Lending in the United States* is a series of state-by-state listings ranking commercial banks' small business lending activities as of June 1994 by looking at such data as the number and dollar value of small business loans outstanding, the dollar value of small business loans relative to total deposits, and several other lending ratios and measures. This analysis is based upon loan data culled from the quarterly Call Reports filed with the federal financial supervisory agencies.

The CRA examination procedures for large retail institutions instruct examiners to determine whether any similarly situated institutions (in terms of size, financial condition, product offerings, and business strategy) serve the same or similar assessment area(s) and would provide relevant information for evaluating the institution's CRA performance. According to the CRA examination procedures, examiners will consider successful

CRA-related product offerings or activities offered by other lenders serving the same or similar assessment area(s). Understanding the market will make it advisable for a bank or thrift to be familiar with the product offerings and activities of competing financial institutions in the institution's assessment area.

The CRA examination procedures for both small institutions and large retail institutions also make clear that regulatory consideration of the performance context involves an element of peer group analysis or the much dreaded market share review of competitive position. Examiners are instructed to obtain relevant demographic, economic, and loan data, to the extent available, on each assessment area under review. The CRA examination procedures for large retail institutions also instruct examiners to consider whether the area has housing costs that are particularly high given area median income.

Supervisory agencies use numbers of housing units, occupied units and owner-occupied units as performance indicators to evaluate market opportunity for housing loans. On a periodic basis, management should review market share in lower-income versus higher-income geographic markets and among different income levels of customer groups (the four income profiles of borrowers), in both cases as a percent of the institution's total lending, loan type by loan type. This should not be an after-the-fact compliance obligation, but part of the loan management function. Performance relative to the peer group is an easy measuring rod that examiners will use to assess an institution's actual performance.

Financial institutions should not regard the new CRA regulations as deliverance from the burden of documenting CRA compliance. The institutions that will achieve the best results under the new CRA rules are those whose approach to CRA compliance is systematic and disciplined. An institution cannot guarantee itself that it will achieve outstanding CRA results obviously. The kind of management control over the planning, execution, monitoring, and correction phases of CRA compliance that results in outstanding CRA performance necessarily requires documentation, perhaps at least as much documentation as institutions generally prepared under the old CRA regulations. The CRA rules underscore the importance of quantitative information as well, which institutions should take pains to gather in order to avoid the circumstance of trying to reverse examiners' findings that may be based on erroneous, misinterpreted, or incomplete data. The demographic information and analysis required under the new rules are not themselves new. The federal financial supervisory agencies adopted the Federal Financial Institutions Examination Council's December 1991 policy statement requiring institutions to conduct an analysis of geographic distribution of loan applications, denials, and approvals, including an analysis of the relationship of geographic distribution to such demographic factors as income levels, percentage of minority population, age of housing stock, number of owner-occupied housing units, and so on.

Now that the new CRA regulations codify and expand upon that 1991 policy statement, virtually all institutions will be exploring quantitative CRA documentation to a degree that they might not have done before, in order to determine (1) which segments of their assessment areas are low- and moderate-income and (2) the extent of the institution's loan penetration in those low- and moderate-income segments of the assessment areas, and in order to conduct various demographic and other analysis necessary to establish an appropriate performance context for the institution.

Loan distribution analysis requires a financial institution's management to have an understanding of the institution's loan distributions to minorities, in minority areas (particularly African-American areas), to low- and moderate-income borrowers, and in low- and moderate-income areas.

Loan distribution analysis has become an essential part not only of fair lending compliance, but CRA compliance as well. Loan distribution analysis is necessary not only to determine whether an institution has been in compliance with the CRA and fair lending laws, but also to help an institution to direct its future compliance efforts. Loan distribution analysis should become an integral part of management deliberations concerning loan marketing and production, rather than being merely an after-the-fact responsibility of the CRA officer to quantify CRA and fair lending compliance. In this way, an institution can assure itself that it is exercising the greatest degree of control over its CRA and fair lending compliance and the outcome of its CRA performance assessment. CRA compliance has not yet reached this level at many (if not most) financial institutions. Loan distribution analysis is still regarded as a compliance responsibility alone, rather than a shared responsibility of those in loan marketing and production who have the greatest degree of actual control over CRA compliance.

The clear lesson that has emerged from fair lending cases and CRA regulation over the past few years is that each and every bank and thrift must ensure (1) that the institution's banking products and services are made available and marketed with equal vigor to each and every sector of the institution's community(ies); (2) that the institution undertakes as a *routine* part of its CRA compliance a careful analysis of the institution's geographic loan distribution (particularly, but not exclusively, an analysis of the institution's home mortgage loan distribution) to identify areas or income groups within the institution's community that are underrepresented; (3) that a similar analysis is undertaken to ascertain whether minorities are underrepresented among the institution's borrowers; and (4) if a pattern of disparate impact emerges from the analysis, that the institution (*a*) be able to account for (explain) why minorities are underrepresented relative to the expected loan distribution and (*b*) take immediate steps to correct the underrepresentation of minorities within the institution's borrower base.

The analysis should be performed for each loan product, for each census tract within an assessment area, for each assessment area and so on, and the analysis should focus on, among other things, distributions of loans to (1) low-income and moderate-income individuals and neighborhoods versus middle- and upper-income borrowers and (2) minority (particularly African-American) borrowers versus white borrowers. A sample format for loan distribution analysis appears in Appendix 1. A final point on the subject of loan distribution analysis is that loan distribution data represent only one half of the equation.

The other half, knowing the demographics and demographic trends in the market(s) in which an institution operates, is at least as important. Without this information, loan distribution analysis can paint a deceptively bad picture, and the institution is deprived of information that would help the institution to customize its product offerings and marketing efforts in low- and moderate-income areas to greatest effect. Some census tracts can, for example, be so underprivileged that there is virtually no opportunity for lending to residents within such a tract, or they can have virtually no sales of residences within a particular time period, preventing any lenders from making home purchase loans in those tracts. Thus, one would like to know such demographic data as the number of owner-occupied housing units in a tract, the median age and value of the housing units, the average or actual number of home sale transactions within a year, the percentage of those that were financed, the percentage of the latter that were financed through mortgage brokers or with government-assistance in some form, and so on.

For most financial institutions in cities across the country, HMDA data show loan denial and acceptance rates for various races and income categories indicating that the institution has a disproportionately high denial rate for African-American applicants versus white applicants. This is a systemic problem. However, the significance of the disparity in white versus black loan denial rates cannot be dismissed. An institution that does not perform the necessary demographic and loan distribution analyses might be more vulnerable to criticism than the institution whose demographic and loan distribution analyses form a basis upon which that institution is able to explain, clarify, or correct an apparently high denial rate for African-Americans.

Aside from gathering marketplace demographic information, an institution should make certain to include its marketing function in CRA compliance efforts. Marketing personnel have every bit as much a role to play in CRA compliance under the revised regulations as do loan production personnel. Those involved in the marketing function should understand the marketplace demographic information that lending officers will also be utilizing. An effective marketing plan based on the demographics of the institution's assessment area is a necessary predicate to performance success. The current state of fair lending regulatory enforcement recognizes that marketing is a necessary stimulus to loan performance.

As a necessary component of CRA compliance, a bank or thrift should stay attuned to developments in the law of CRA and fair lending. Particularly in the recent past, there have been a number of developments in these areas that are of special significance, including the U.S. Department of Justice consent decrees with Chevy Chase Federal Savings Bank ("Chevy Chase") and Decatur Federal Savings and Loan Association ("Decatur"). These decrees have a number of common elements, which offer insight on an issue that has, since the CRA was adopted in 1977, made CRA compliance a very uncertain undertaking: precisely (or as precisely as possible) what sorts of activities must be undertaken in order to comply with the CRA and to what extent must they be undertaken? Although the consent decrees are nominally based upon fair lending laws, fair lending principles are a critical part of CRA compliance, and an explicit consideration in the CRA rating process.

In both the Chevy Chase and Decatur consent decrees, Chevy Chase and Decatur were required to place 960 column inches of advertising in a one-year period in minority-oriented written media. The decrees also established specific goals for related activities, including adoption of point-of-sale marketing materials for CRA-related lending products and participation in mortgage lending fairs and seminars for brokers active in African-American communities. Financial institutions should regard the terms of the consent decrees as *indicative of* (as opposed to conclusive statements of) the kind and amount of activities that are necessary for fair lending and CRA compliance. This offers specific guidance in a subject for which there had been virtually none, apart from the admonition that an institution must not discriminate on the basis of race or other prohibited factors, an admonition banks routinely adopt as corporate policy.

The guidance offered by the consent decrees is particularly welcome at a time when, as now, the treatment by an institution of issues such as disparate impact of loan distributions in white versus black segments of a community and divergent loan denial rates for black versus white applicants has become an important part of CRA compliance. These are issues as to which obedience to the admonition against discrimination offers little or no assurance of favorable results, as disparate loan distributions and loan denial rates are systemic concerns limited to no one institution and no one bank or thrift officer. It is especially helpful, therefore, to have specific guidance in this developing and uncertain aspect of fair lending and CRA compliance.

Banks who do not have the kind or amount of loan production to minorities that they seek may well be surprised when they conduct a critical review of their marketing activities. Every bank, and particularly institutions that are the largest residential mortgage lenders in their markets, should consider how the institution's print advertising, measured by column inches, in minority-oriented written media compares to that required of Chevy Chase and Decatur. Because Chevy Chase and Decatur were also subject to requirements concerning the holding of mortgage lending fairs, a bank should also consider how often it participates in mortgage lending fairs and seminars held for the benefit of minority and low- and moderate-income persons and brokers and other parties with an interest in those communities. Moreover, a bank that has developed a number of special CRA-related lending products must consider how vigorously the institution advertises in minority and low- and moderate-income communities, through print, radio and television media, as well as by means of point-of-sale marketing materials.

A reason to continue documenting CRA compliance is that there must be value in being able to demonstrate that the institution tried to achieve outstanding CRA results, even if the institution's efforts were not entirely successful. This will be the unfortunate position of many institutions. It is axiomatic that in a world of competition somebody wins, but everybody else has to lose. Some institutions will earn outstanding CRA ratings from their regulators, and some of them will do so from one evaluation to the next. Many, however, will be runners-up in this beauty pageant, earning ratings of satisfactory. Just as surely as some institutions will earn ratings of outstanding, others will be rated needs-to-improve and there will surely be some tagged with the lowest rating of all—"substantial noncompliance."

The universe of creditworthy low- and moderate-income borrowers is finite. If Bank A and Bank B compete year in and year out for the same low- or moderate-income customer in the assessment area they share, and year after year the customer borrows from Bank A because unlike Bank B, Bank A can afford to make a loan to the customer on terms far more favorable than prevailing market conditions would allow, it is true enough that Bank A can rest assured of a satisfactory rating at least, and perhaps a rating of outstanding, documentation or no documentation. But what does Bank B have to show for its CRA compliance efforts? Bank B will not have the desired results. Thus, if Bank B does not have documentary proof that it tried to identify and serve all low- and moderate-income persons in the institution's assessment area, then Bank B has nothing to show for its efforts to comply with CRA, regardless of how substantial those efforts may have been.

Further compounding this problem is that many of the large institutions have the resources to enter into substantial CRA commitments with municipalities and community and consumer groups, which resources smaller institutions simply do not have in nearly the same degree. As the CRA rulemaking itself acknowledged, many such commitments have been made, resulting in the infusion of "tens of billions of dollars" into low- and moderate-income areas.[3] In addition to money that has already flowed into communities as a result of these commitments, billions of dollars more are committed over a number of years that varies from one commitment to the next. The effect of these commitments is making it more difficult for smaller institutions to (1) make significant gains in market share in areas that are the beneficiaries of the commitments and (2) to do so on terms that are acceptable, whether in terms of adequacy of return or probability of repayment. Smaller institutions simply cannot compete with the typical features of the lending commitments made by the larger institutions, nor do they have the margin for error with respect to repayment probabilities that larger institutions have. The loan terms featured in the many special lending commitments made by large institutions, particularly in connection with acquisitions, are so favorable to consumers that a rational consumer in the beneficiary group would not choose a mortgage product, for example, offered by a smaller institution at prevailing market rates and terms over a similar product made available on extremely favorable rates and terms through the lending commitment.

There is only a finite amount of creditworthy consumer demand in low- and moderate-income markets, and in any market for that matter. In the gathering of marketplace demographic information to portray an institution's performance context, an institution should attempt to describe the extent to which large lending commitments have absorbed and will increasingly absorb that limited demand. In the view of many smaller financial institutions, such commitments will inevitably tip the competitive balance more in favor of large institutions than it already is, particularly in favor of those large institutions that have already entered into sizable CRA lending commitments. This competitive bias is quite apart from, and in addition to, the revised CRA rules' bias in favor of those institutions that already happen to have sizable market shares in low- and moderate-income areas.

While it is natural that community activists or customers may write public file comment letters that are critical of an institution's CRA performance, financial institutions should give thought to encouraging "friends" of the institution to write public file CRA comment letters that extol the institution's CRA performance. In this way, when examiners review the institution's public file and any comments received by the institution, the institution can document that its CRA performance serves the community's credit needs. Additionally, a well-written public file CRA comment letter can favorably influence an examiner's perception of the institution's performance context.

While the financial institution should not write the public file comment letter on behalf of the institution's customer, several pointers should be provided to the customer writing the public file comment letter. Providing a sample script or summarizing key points which should be addressed in the public file comment letter could be advisable. The comment letter should make clear how the institution's activity or service helps to meet the community's credit needs. That should be the primary purpose of the letter. Additionally, the letter should contain a notation directing the institution to place a copy of the letter in the institution's CRA public file comment letters. So that the letter does not look too "canned" or "staged," the public file comment letter could even contain a suggestion for improvement (obviously one hopes of a mild and self-serving nature). A sample public file comment letter submitted by a "friend" of a community bank appears as Appendix 2.

[3] THREE TEST CRITERIA FOR LARGE BANKS

The CRA performance of large institutions—institutions with $250 million or more in assets and institutions, regardless of asset size, owned by holding companies with total bank and thrift institution assets of $1 billion or more—will be evaluated under three tests:

1. The lending test.
2. The investment test.
3. The service test.

If a large institution does not wish to be evaluated under the large institution criteria, the institution may request to be designated as a wholesale or limited purpose institution, or the institution may be approved for evaluation under a strategic plan.

For institutions other than (a) small banks or thrifts who fail to select large institution evaluation, (b) wholesale institutions, (c) limited purpose institutions, or (d) institutions selecting the strategic plan assessment option, the appropriate federal financial supervisory agency will evaluate an institution's lending performance based on the following criteria:

1. The number and amount of home mortgage, small business, small farm, and consumer loans, if applicable, in the institution's assessment area(s). Examiners will identify loans to be evaluated by reviewing the HMDA and CRA disclosure statements, interim HMDA and CRA data collected, a sample of consumer loans (if a substantial majority of the institution's business is comprised of consumer loans), and other loan information provided by the institution.
2. The geographic distribution of these loans, including the proportion of the institution's total loans within the

assessment area(s), dispersion of loans within the assessment area(s), and the number and amount of loans in different income level geographies in the assessment area(s). An institution is not expected to lend evenly throughout or to every geography in its assessment area. Rather, an institution's lending pattern should not exhibit conspicuous gaps that are not adequately explained by the performance context. The CRA examination procedures for large retail institutions require examiners to consider the number and dollar volume of home purchase, home refinancing, and home improvement loans, respectively, in each geography compared to the number of one- to four-family-occupied units in each geography. Examiners are also required to consider the number and dollar volume of multifamily loans in each geography compared to the number of multifamily structures in each geography, and the number and dollar volume of small business and small farm loans in each geography compared to the number of small businesses/farms in each geography.

If there are groups of contiguous geographies within the institution's assessment area with abnormally low penetration, the CRA examination procedures provide that the examiner may determine if an analysis of the institution's performance compared to other lenders for home mortgage loans (using reported HMDA data) and for small business and small farm loans (using data provided by lenders subject to CRA) would provide an insight into the institution's lack of performance in those areas. The geographic distribution criterion is probably more important in urban assessment areas with the full range of different income level geographies.

3. The distribution, particularly in the institution's assessment area(s), of the institution's home mortgage, small business, small farm, and consumer loans, if applicable, based on borrower characteristics, including the number and amount of home mortgage loans to

individuals of the four different income levels; small business and small farm loans to businesses and farms with gross annual revenues of $1 million or less; small business and small farm loans by loan amount at origination; and consumer loans, if applicable, to low-, moderate-, middle-, and upper-income individuals. The CRA examination procedures require examiners to consider the percentage of an institution's total home mortgage loans and consumer loans, if included in the evaluation, to the four income profiles compared to the percentage of the population within the assessment area who are low, moderate, middle, and upper income. The same concept applies relative to small business lending. The institution's number and amount of loans to such borrowers will be compared to the total reported number and amount of loans to such borrowers within that assessment area. In an assessment area without pronounced different income level geographies, loan distribution based on borrower characteristics is more important than the geographic distribution criterion previously identified in no. 2 above.

4. The institution's community development lending, including the number and amount of community development loans, and their complexity and innovativeness.

5. The institution's use of innovative or flexible lending practices in a safe and sound manner to address the credit needs of low- or moderate-income individuals or geographies. The CRA examination procedures instruct examiners to consider the degree to which innovative loan products or products with more flexible terms have been successful, including the number and dollar volume of loans originated during the review period.

The CRA regulations do not impose any reporting requirements for consumer lending. However, if an examiner determines that a "substantial majority" of an institution's business is consumer lending, and the institution has not elected to provide consumer loan data, the examiner will evaluate consumer lending in the lending test by analyzing an appropriate sample of the institution's consumer loan portfolio. At an October 19, 1995, CRA teleconference conducted by the four federal financial supervisory agencies to explain the revised CRA regulations, a question and answer regulator response indicated that both the number and volume of consumer loans will be used to determine if there is a "substantial majority" of consumer loans within an institution's portfolio. In response to questions posed at the teleconference, regulators refused to confirm that any number, including 51 percent, 52 percent, or even 80 percent, constitutes a "substantial majority." Until several years have passed under the revised CRA regulations and until experience in the form of available public performance evaluations suggests otherwise, institutions might find it prudent to assume that greater than 50 percent of total loan assets will constitute "a substantial majority."

The relative weight of the different lending categories (home mortgage, small business, and small farm lending, and consumer lending if considered) will be determined by examiners based on the institution's performance context. According to supplemental information appearing in the Federal Register for the final CRA rulemaking, there is no fixed formula for the relative weight of the different categories. Just as in George Orwell's novel *Animal Farm* some animals were more equal than others, so too will certain types of loans informally rank higher in the pecking order of CRA theology. Loan products developed to meet the credit needs of low-income borrowers will probably receive most favorable evaluation. Some national and superregional banking organizations are now offering no-down-payment, no-closing-cost loans to low-income consumers. To the extent a lender develops special loan products for low-income customers not offered by the secondary market agencies, the institution can be assured of receiving more favorable consideration for these types of loans. Next in the pecking order of favorable CRA consideration by examiners are loans in low-income census tracts, followed by loans that qualify as community development loans under the CRA regulations.

The CRA regulation assesses an institution's use of innovative or flexible lending practices in a safe and sound manner to address the credit needs of low- and moderate-income individuals or geographies. According to supplemental information appearing in the Federal Register for the final CRA rulemaking, an innovative practice is one that serves low- and moderate-income creditworthy borrowers in new ways or serves groups of creditworthy borrowers not previously served by the institution. Both innovative practices and flexible practices are favorably considered. The supplemental information appearing in the Federal Register for the final CRA rulemaking also indicated that a practice ceases to be innovative if its use is widespread; nonetheless, the supplemental information also notes that such a practice may receive consideration if it is a flexible practice. An institution need not provide lending data connected with a practice in order to receive consideration. For example, an examiner could consider an institution's secured credit card program as a flexible lending practice even though the institution has not provided its credit card loan data for evaluation under the other criteria of the lending test.

A rating of outstanding or satisfactory cannot be achieved without at least a rating of "low satisfactory" on the lending test (a rating of outstanding cannot be achieved without at least a "high satisfactory" on the lending test). Conversely, an institution cannot receive worse than an overall "satisfactory" rating if it receives an outstanding rating on the lending test.

At the institution's option, affiliate lending or community development consortium lending will be considered by the appropriate federal financial supervisory agency if the bank or thrift provides data on such loans pursuant to Section .42(e) of the CRA regulation (the data reporting obligation to the regulatory agency).

The staffs of the four federal financial supervisory agencies are presently developing written guidance to assist in resolving interpretive questions under the revised CRA regulations. OCC Interpretive Letter No. 714, dated March 25, 1996, indicates that a bank that invests in a community development financial institution (CDFI) could elect to receive credit under the CRA "lending test" for its pro rata share of community development loans made by the CDFI. The bank would receive consideration for the amount of community development loans made as a result of its investment in the CDFI and for the amount of any such loan that it purchases from the CDFI.

For other than (1) small banks or thrifts who fail to elect large institution evaluation, (2) wholesale institutions, (3) limited purpose institutions, or (4) institutions selecting the strategic plan assessment option, the appropriate federal financial supervisory agency will evaluate an institution's investment performance based on the following criteria:

1. The dollar amount of qualified investments.
2. The innovativeness or complexity of qualified investments.
3. The responsiveness of qualified investments to credit and community development needs.
4. The degree to which the qualified investments are not routinely provided by private investors.

Although Chapter 4 identified examples of qualified investment, the difficulty that many community financial institutions have attaining qualified investments makes it appropriate to repeat how restrictive the examples of qualified investments are:

1. In state and municipal obligations that specifically support affordable housing or other community development. Investments in municipal bonds designed primarily to finance community development generally are qualified and need not be housing related. Housing-related municipal bonds must primarily address affordable housing (including multifamily rental housing) in order to qualify. Investments in untargeted municipal bonds and standard mortgage-backed securities will not qualify. Investment in Federal Home Loan Bank stock does not qualify.
2. To support or develop facilities that promote community development in low- and moderate-income areas or for low- and moderate-income individuals, such as day care facilities.
3. In projects eligible for low-income housing tax credits.

4. To not-for-profit organizations serving low- and moderate-income housing or other community development needs, such as home counseling, home maintenance counseling, credit counseling, and other financial services education.

5. In or to organize supporting activities essential to the capacity of low- and moderate-income individuals or areas to utilize credit or to sustain economic development.

For most financial institutions, the investment department or investment function has been, at best, a distant backwater of CRA compliance. It goes without saying that employees in the investment department must receive adequate training so that they can identify opportunities for the institution to make CRA-related investments that will receive favorable evaluation as qualified investments. Depending on the division of responsibility within a financial institution, such training should probably also be extended to loan officers so that they can appropriately structure qualified investment opportunities in conjunction with the institution's lending opportunities. For example, for many, if not most, financial institutions, projects eligible for low-income tax credits would be administered by the institution's loan department, rather than the institution's investment department.

Recognizing how restrictive the definition of qualified investment is, the staffs of the four federal financial supervisory agencies are developing written guidance to assist institutions in plotting activities and investments subject to favorable CRA evaluation. For example, the OTS chief counsel issued a letter, dated March 28, 1996, that Neighborhood Housing Services of America (NHSA) securities backed by residential loan pools will be considered qualified investments for thrifts. Over time, the regulators can be expected to issue interpretive letters opining as to whether certain specialized investments satisfy the qualified investment criteria. For example, OCC Interpretive Letter No. 715, dated April 2, 1996, provides that an investment in a geographically specific private placement debt securities fund could receive positive CRA consideration as a "qualified investment" if, collectively, the underlying debt securities primarily promote community development activities. In this regard, a mortgage-backed security is considered a "qualified investment" only if the entire security primarily funds affordable housing for low- or moderate-income individuals. Investments promoting education are "qualified investments" only if they are targeted to low- or moderate-income individuals.

An institution whose putative qualified investment has no ready match in the laundry list of recognized qualified investments is well advised to consider any written guidance promulgated by the staffs of the four federal financial supervisory agencies that supplements the CRA rulemaking process.

Examiners should consider a savings association's limited investment authority in evaluating performance under the investment test. A savings association that has few or no qualified investments may still be considered to be performing adequately under the investment test if, for example, the institution is particularly effective in responding to the community's credit needs through community development lending activities.

Given the difficulty that many financial institutions, particularly thrift institutions, will have in engaging in activities that would be favorably evaluated under the investment test, an action plan for involving the giving program in CRA compliance should be considered. A significant portion of an institution's donations and grants can support community development (affordable housing, community services for low- and moderate-income people, revitalization, or small business development projects). Reallocation of the charitable contribution budget can be a simple means to achieve some qualified investments for purposes of the investment test. The CRA examination procedures confirm that examiners will consider qualifying grants, donations, or in-kind contributions of property as qualified investments.

At an institution's option, the federal financial supervisory agency will consider, in its assessment of an institution's investment performance, a qualified investment made by an affiliate of the bank or thrift, if the qualified investment is not claimed by any other institution.

The service test evaluates an institution's record of helping to meet the credit needs of the institution's assessment area(s), by analyzing both the availability and effectiveness of an institution's branching network and service delivery systems. The test is divided into an analysis of an institution's retail banking services and an institution's community development services.

For other than (a) small banks or thrifts who fail to select large institution evaluation, (b) wholesale institutions, (c) limited purpose institutions, or (d) institutions electing the strategic plan assessment option, the appropriate federal financial supervisory agency will evaluate an institution's retail service performance (the first prong of service test performance) based on the following criteria:

1. The current distribution of the institution's branches among the four different income geographies. The service delivery system should not exhibit conspicuous gaps in accessibility, particularly to low- or moderate-income areas or individuals, unless the gaps are adequately explained by the performance context.

2. In the context of the distribution of the institution's branches, the institution's record of opening and closing branches, particularly in low- and moderate-income geographies or primarily serving low- or moderate-income individuals.

3. The availability and effectiveness of alternate systems for delivering retail banking services (e.g., ATMs, including those not owned by the institution, banking by phone or computer, loan production offices, bank-at-work programs, and bank-by-mail programs) in low- and moderate-income geographies and to low- and moderate-income individuals. Note that the inclusion of ATMs has been limited to the extent that they provide effective services to low- and moderate-income areas.

4. The range of services provided in low-, moderate-, middle-, and upper-income geographies and the degree to which the services are tailored to meet the needs of those geographies. The CRA examination procedures for large retail institutions require examiners to consider

the degree to which services are tailored to the convenience and needs of each geography (e.g., extended business hours, including weekends, evenings, or by appointment; and providing bilingual services in specific geographies). Thus, for example, a bank would receive favorable evaluation for employing Spanish-speaking tellers or loan officers in Hispanic markets.

Many bankers believe that the service test will require an institution to locate branches where the institution might not otherwise choose to do so. The preamble to the CRA regulation made clear "the test does not require an institution to expand its branch network or operate unprofitable branches."[4] Further, the preamble made clear that an institution's branches and other service delivery systems "need not be accessible to every part of an institution's assessment area," but cautions there should not be "conspicuous gaps in accessibility, particularly to low- or moderate-income areas" unless such a gap is "adequately explained by the performance context" (e.g., no housing in a manufacturing area)."[5]

Notwithstanding the preamble language that appeared in the final CRA rulemaking, institutions do feel conflicting pressures to establish branches where they might otherwise not choose to do so. For example, the precedent established by the August 22, 1994, consent decree between the Justice Department and Chevy Chase Federal Savings Bank ("Chevy Chase") makes many financial institution managements believe that an institution must seek to gain as much market share in minority communities as the institution does in nonminority communities. In the first case of its kind, the U.S. Department of Justice alleged that the largest thrift institution in the Washington, D.C., area, Chevy Chase and its B. F. Saul Mortgage Company subsidiary, violated the Fair Housing Act (FHA) and the Equal Credit Opportunity Act (ECOA) by marketing mortgage loans only in predominantly nonminority areas, a practice that the Justice Department characterized as redlining. The Justice Department expanded its definition of mortgage lending discrimination under these two fair lending statutes to include the failure of financial institutions to locate branches and to market mortgages in minority neighborhoods.

Through this consent decree, the Justice Department sent a clear message that lenders must seek to gain as much market share in minority communities as they do in nonminority neighborhoods. It should be noted that the complaint filed by the Justice Department mentions only violation of the FHA and the ECOA and not the CRA. To remedy Chevy Chase's alleged refusal to make its services available in predominantly African-American neighborhoods, Chevy Chase agreed to open branches and mortgage origination offices in the "redlined" areas. To many lenders the *Chevy Chase* consent decree stands for the proposition that if there is market share inequality in terms of loan originations to minorities versus nonminorities, the institution must seek to remedy that disparity by locating branches and marketing mortgage loans in minority neighborhoods to the same extent as they are offered in nonminority areas. There is no clear answer to the tension between enforcement of the fair lending laws and CRA enforcement. The tension between enforcement of the fair lending laws and CRA service test requirements as to branch-siting decisions is of greatest concern to financial institutions that can be considered as the lender with the largest market share.

Relative to the fourth item serving as the basis for evaluation of an institution's retail banking services (the range of services provided in low-, moderate-, middle-, and upper-income geographies), all branch personnel and other customer service personnel should receive training in the services offered by the institution. Because CRA compliance now affects all areas of an institution's operations, personnel must be cross-trained so that deposit-side personnel are familiar with the basics of the bank's lending operations, and loan officers are conversely familiar with the bank's deposit-side operations. To the extent an institution is deficient in its employee training, misunderstandings with customers are likely to surface. Such misunderstandings, if held on the part of protected classes under the fair lending laws, can produce fair lending complaints which, at best, involve a tremendous amount of work to remedy erroneous impressions or, at worst, have an adverse impact on an institution's CRA performance.

Community development services (the second prong of service test performance) are evaluated by the federal financial supervisory agency pursuant to the following criteria:

1. The extent to which a bank or savings association provides community development services.
2. The innovativeness and responsiveness of community development services.

What is "innovative" is always in evolution. What was considered innovative at the preceding examination will not necessarily be innovative at a current examination two years later.

No area of bank operations is less accustomed to CRA compliance than the retail delivery system and a bank's deposit function. Bank management should include the head of the savings area and the person in charge of the retail branch and ATM delivery system in CRA compliance. Because retail service channels and performance cannot be radically changed on an overnight basis, it is all the more important that management be particularly sensitive to opportunities to provide community development services. Providing home buyer counseling seminars, participating in school savings programs (also known as "kiddie banking" programs), and offering low-cost checking accounts or free government check cashing are services offered by many institutions and ones that any institution should evaluate for possible inclusion under the institution's record of providing community development services.

[4] SMALL BANK PERFORMANCE STANDARDS

Recognizing that regulatory and examination burdens can be disproportionately greater on smaller institutions, the new CRA regulations establish a streamlined assessment method for small institutions. A small institution is a bank or thrift that, as of December 31 of either of the prior two calendar years, had total assets of less than $250 million and was independent or that was an affiliate of a holding company that, as of December 31 of either of the prior two calendar years, had total banking and thrift assets of less than $1 billion. In addition, the CRA regulations clarify that growth during the year does not change the eligibility for the streamlined test. If an institution qualifies as of the end of the prior calendar year for the streamlined test, the institution is examined as a small institution.

If a small institution does not wish to be evaluated under the small institution performance standards, the institution may request to be designated as a wholesale or limited purpose institution, the institution may be approved for evaluation under a strategic plan, or the institution can request evaluation under the large bank performance standards.

While the revised CRA regulations contain five performance criteria for small banks, the small bank performance standards essentially focus on lending performance (three of the five criteria are part of the lending test for large institutions). The new small business and agricultural loan data recordkeeping requirements for larger institutions do not apply to smaller institutions.

A federal financial supervisory agency evaluates a small bank's record of helping to meet the credit needs of the institution's assessment area(s) pursuant to the following criteria:

1. The institution's loan-to-deposit ratio, adjusted for seasonal variation and, as appropriate, other lending-related activities, such as loan originations for sale to the secondary markets, community development loans, or qualified investments.

2. The percentage of loans and, as appropriate, other lending-related activities located in the institution's assessment area(s). According to the CRA examination procedures, less than a majority of lending within the assessment area represents unsatisfactory performance.

3. The institution's record of lending to borrowers of different income levels and, as appropriate, engaging in other lending-related activities for borrowers of different income levels and businesses and farms of different sizes.

4. The geographic distribution of the institution's loans.

5. The institution's record of taking action, if warranted, in response to written complaints about the institution's performance in helping to meet credit needs in its assessment area(s).

Lending is evaluated on an originations basis with consideration given for loan sales. A small bank or thrift is not required to conduct any loan distribution analysis or to geocode its loans if the institution does not do so already. Regulators have made clear that geocoding will be done by examiners as part of the streamlined examination. As a practical matter, an institution should keep a record of loan originations since the previous examination, and should keep information on census tract data in the institution's assessment area. Although institutions are not required to keep such data in electronic format, examiners may ask for data in an electronic format if such information is available in this format.

The preparatory work a small institution performs relative to loan distribution analysis will be the means to attain an examination restricted in examiner scope and time. The results under the lending criteria noted above are not absolutes, but rather will be evaluated by reference to a performance context. Thus, the institution that has the best grasp of its performance context and that is most able to communicate that to its regulator will probably be the one judged as having the best results.

Relative to the level of preparatory work an institution completes to describe the institution's performance context, it is instructive to look at performance evaluations of small institutions completed during 1996 by the federal financial supervisory agencies. Performance evaluations for small institutions routinely include a description of the population and number of households within the assessment area. The description of the assessment area also identifies the median household income and the median family income with stratification by income level category for the aggregate number of block numbering areas and census tracts. In addition to understanding the block numbering areas and census tracts within the assessment area in terms of the racial composition of the assessment area and the four income profiles, the institution should also understand the number of residents who are low and moderate income, even though there might not necessarily be low- and moderate-income areas within the institution's assessment area. An understanding of the performance context also requires the institution to be able to identify the nature of the housing stock (whether owner occupied, one- to four-family dwellings, mobile homes, rental housing stock, and the number of building permits issued for single family residential and multifamily units). The institution should also know the median housing value in its market, as well as the average rent. Identification of the performance context also requires the institution to understand and to be able to identify the predominant industries within the assessment area, major employers, and unemployment statistics within the assessment area. Although this will be unfamiliar territory to most financial institutions, the U.S. Census Bureau does provide employment data by number of establishments, with a breakdown by the number of employees for different staffing levels (1–49 employees, 50–499 employees, 500 or more employees).

Small bank examination procedures require examiners to sample loans from the past six months, the previous year, and the prior CRA examination. The universe of loans sampled by examiners must include at least 50 of each major type. The data fields to be reviewed by examiners include loan number, loan type or code, loan amount, loan date, borrower's name, borrower's income or business revenue if applicable, street address, city, state, zip code and MSA, county, and census tract or block numbering area information. With this information, examiners will be able to conduct the income and revenue distribution of credit contemplated by the third performance criterion. Small bank examination procedures require examiners to use data, if available, about borrower income (for individuals) or revenues (for businesses) to determine the distribution of loans by borrower income and by business revenues. Examiners will identify categories of borrowers by income or business revenues for which the bank has little or no loan penetration. If sufficient geographic or income/revenue data are not available to conduct an analysis of the distribution of credit, examiners will consider alternatives such as analyzing geographic distribution by street address rather than geography. If there are geographies or income categories of low penetration, examiners will form conclusions about the reasons in light of the institution's performance context.

Once the lending picture of a smaller institution is developed, the examiner will look to the loan-to-deposit ratio for "reasonableness." The loan-to-deposit ratio is averaged over four quarters in order to smooth seasonal fluctuations. Because the industry objected so strongly to the 60 percent "bright line" loan-to-deposit ratio set forth in the proposed CRA regulations, examiners will evaluate "reasonableness" in terms of the institution's performance context, its lending performance, and community development loans and qualified investments when determining whether or not the reasonableness standard is being met. In particular, examiners will evaluate the loan-to-deposit ratio by reference to capacity of other similarly situated institutions in the assessment area. If the loan-to-deposit ratio does not appear reasonable, examiners will give additional consideration to the number and dollar volume of loans sold to the secondary market, as well as to the innovativeness or complexity of community development loans and qualified investments.

According to remarks made at an October 19, 1995, CRA teleconference held by the FDIC, the OTS, the OCC, and the FRB to explain the revised CRA regulations, stronger performance on some of the above five criteria can compensate for weaker performance on other of the five criteria.

A small institution is not required to meet the investment and service criteria applied to larger institutions. A small institution may use activity to qualify under either test to boost the institution's rating to "outstanding." While investment and service activities may raise a "satisfactory" to an "outstanding," such activities will not cause a "needs to improve" to become a "satisfactory." The CRA examination procedures for small institutions confirm that at an institution's option, the examiner will consider the institution's performance in making qualified investments and in providing services that enhance credit availability in the institution's assessment area(s) in

T A B L E 5–2

Small Institution Performance Evaluation

Small Institution Assessment Criteria	(Name of Financial Institution) Performance Levels		
	Exceeds Standards for Satisfactory Performance	Meets Standards for Satisfactory Performance	Does Not Meet Standards for Satisfactory Performance
Loan-to-deposit ratio			
Lending in assessment area			
Lending to borrowers of different incomes and to businesses of different sizes			
Geographic distribution of loans			
Response to complaints			

order to determine whether the institution merits an outstanding rating.

The public evaluation provided by a small institution's federal financial supervisory agency will include a table to disclose the institution's performance under the streamlined examination criteria that will be similar to Table 5–2.

Relative to the last item in Table 5–2 serving as a basis for CRA performance evaluation (the institution's response to written complaints, if any, about the institution's performance in helping to meet the credit needs of the institution's assessment area), performance evaluations completed to date under the revised CRA regulations indicate that an institution is well advised to have a written fair lending policy and review procedures to ensure consistent application of the institution's lending policy. Institutions should also make certain that training for compliance with fair lending laws is conducted periodically and is documented. Written CRA performance evaluations completed through the first four months of 1996 note such process-oriented items favorably.

[5] DATA COLLECTION AND REPORTING

The CRA regulations' data collection and reporting requirements, a curse of large bank status, are not required for small banks unless they elect to be evaluated under the lending, investment, and service tests by which non-small banks are evaluated. Of course, such small institutions, if subject to HMDA data collection requirements, remain subject to such HMDA requirements independent of any CRA-imposed data collection and reporting requirement.

To illustrate how growth in asset size of a small bank may affect the institution's data collection and data reporting requirements, consider the following example:

Date	Institution's Asset Size	Data Collection Required for Following Calendar Year?
12/31/94	$240 million	No
12/31/95	260 million	No
12/31/96	230 million	No
12/31/97	280 million	No
12/31/98	260 million	Yes, beginning 1/01/99

Tricky coverage issues apply to merging institutions. To illustrate the data collection and reporting responsibilities of merging institutions, consider three scenarios of data collection responsibilities for the calendar year of a merger and subsequent data reporting responsibilities:

a. Two institutions are exempt from CRA collection and reporting requirements because of asset size. The institutions merge. No data collection is required for the year in which the merger takes place regardless of the resulting asset size.[6] Data collection would begin after two consecutive years in which the combined institution had year end banking and thrift assets of at least $1 billion.[7]

b. Institution A, an institution required to collect and report the data, and Institution B, an exempt institution, merge. Institution A is the surviving institution. For the year of the merger, data collection is required for Institution A's transactions.[8] Data collection is optional for the transactions of the previously exempt institution.[9] For the following year, all transactions of the surviving institution must be collected and reported.[10]

c. Two institutions that each are required to collect and report the data merge. Data collection is required for the entire year of the merger and for subsequent years so long as the surviving institution is not exempt.[11] The surviving institution may file either a consolidated submission or separate submissions for the year of the merger but must file a consolidated report for subsequent years.[12]

The data collection requirement of the regulation obliges certain banks to collect, and maintain in machine readable form until the completion of the institution's next CRA examination, the following information for each small business or small farm loan (in either case defined as a loan to a business whose annual revenues were $1 million or less in the preceding year) originated or purchased:

1. A unique number or alpha-numeric symbol that can be used to identify the relevant loan file.
2. The loan amount at origination.
3. The loan location.
4. An indicator of whether the loan was to a business or farm with gross annual revenues of $1 million or less.

An institution will be evaluated on the accuracy of interim CRA loan data collected by it.

For purposes of indicating whether a small business borrower had gross annual revenues of $1 million or less, an institution should generally rely on the revenues that the institution considered in making its credit decision. Question and answer guidance provided by the federal financial supervisory agencies indicates that in the case of affiliated businesses, such as a parent corporation or its subsidiary, if the institution considered the revenues of the entity's parent or a subsidiary corporation of the parent as well, then the institution would combine the revenues of both corporations to determine whether the revenues would be $1 million or less.[13] Alternatively, if the institution considered the revenues of only the entity to which the loan is actually extended, the institution should rely solely upon whether gross annual revenues are above or below $1 million for that entity.[14] However, if the institution considered and relied on revenues or income of a cosigner or guarantor that is not an affiliate of the borrower, the institution should not adjust the borrower's revenues for reporting purposes.[15]

Institutions subject to data collection and reporting must report annually by March 1 to the appropriate federal financial supervisory agency in machine readable form the following data for the prior calendar year:

1. Small business and small farm loan data. For each geography in which the institution originated or purchased a small business or small farm loan, the aggregate number and amount of loans
   a. with an amount at origination of $100,000 or less.
   b. with an amount at origination of more than $100,000 but less than or equal to $250,000.
   c. with an amount at origination of more than $250,000.
   d. to businesses and farms with gross annual revenues of $1 million or less (using revenues considered by the institution in making its credit decision).
2. Community development loan data. The aggregate number and aggregate amount of community development loans originated or purchased.
3. Home mortgage loans (only required for institutions subject to HMDA reporting). The location of each home mortgage loan application, origination, or purchase outside the MSAs in which the institution has a home or branch office or outside any MSA.

The FRB is handling the processing of the reports for all of the federal financial supervisory agencies. The reports should be submitted in a prescribed electronic format on a timely basis. The mailing address for submitting these reports is:

Attention: CRA Processing
Board of Governors of the Federal Reserve System
1709 New York Avenue, NW
5th Floor
Washington, D.C. 20006

The first time data must be reported is March 1, 1997, for data collected in calendar year 1996.

Because a lender's recognition of a community development loan is not based on automation, as is the case, for example, with respect to home mortgage loans subject to HMDA reporting, a financial institution is well advised to develop procedures instructing loan officers in recognizing and claiming credit for the origination of community development loans. Recognition of a community development loan involves considerable judgment. Failure to automate the recognition of community development loans at the time of origination will probably result in many financial institutions failing to claim credit for the origination of loans that in fact are community development loans. Given the importance of community development lending to lending performance evaluation, few financial institutions can afford not to have all community development loans recognized as such by examiners.

Measuring the originated amount on a line of credit involves some complexity. Lines of credit are considered originated at the time the line is approved or increased, and an increase is considered a new origination. Generally, the full amount of the credit line (or in the case of an increase in an existing line, the amount of the increase) is the amount that is considered originated. Although some lines of credit may be for both home improvement and other purposes, only the amount that is considered to be for home improvement purposes is reported as a home improvement loan under HMDA. Lines of credit are considered in assessing an institution's lending activity in all applicable loan types. Therefore, where a portion of a line of credit is reported under HMDA and another portion meets the definition either of a "small business loan" or a "consumer loan," the full amount of the line of credit should be reported as a small business loan or collected as a consumer loan, as appropriate, and the agencies will also consider as a home mortgage loan the portion of the credit line that is reported under HMDA. The CRA regulations contain an option for lenders also to provide data on loans outstanding, which may, in certain circumstances, enhance an examiner's understanding of an institution's performance. Institutions may also provide information on letters of credit and commitments, as well as any other loan information for examiner consideration.

For purposes of the CRA data collection and reporting requirements, an extension of the maturity of an existing loan, without a new credit decision, is a *renewal,* and is not considered a loan origination. Therefore, institutions should not collect and report data on small business and small farm loan renewals.

The CRA regulation also provides for optional data collection of consumer loans. A bank or thrift may collect and maintain data in machine readable form for consumer loans originated or purchased by that institution for consideration under the lending test. An institution may maintain data for one or more categories of consumer loans. The five categories of consumer loans are specified in Chapter 4 of this book and Section .12(k) of the CRA regulation of each federal financial supervisory agency. If the institution maintains data for loans in a certain category, the institution must maintain data for all loans originated or purchased within that category. The data must include:

1. A unique number or alpha-numeric symbol that can be used to identify the relevant loan file.
2. The loan amount at origination or purchase.
3. The loan location.
4. The gross annual income of the borrower that the institution considered in making its credit decision.

An interpretative ruling from the OCC provides guidance on CRA data collection requirements in the context of student lending. River Forest Bancorp, a multibank holding company whose subsidiaries have sizable student loan portfolios, sought guidance on how examiners would treat student loans in a bank's CRA evaluation. The OCC interpretative ruling indicated that since student loans fall under the "other unsecured" category, a lender reporting student loans would have to track and report all the institution's other unsecured consumer loans.

Given that the data collection and reporting imposes tremendous work and possibly even liability for inaccurate data, it would be surprising if great numbers of financial institutions choose to volunteer for optional data collection on consumer loans. An institution whose lending performance for other categories of loans might be considered deficient could conclude that reporting consumer loans represents the institution's only avenue for satisfactory lending performance, particularly if the consumer lending demonstrated strength in consumer lending for low- to moderate-income borrowers.

As noted, errors can easily be made in data collection. Consider the following example. Assume a financial institution chose optional data collection and maintenance relative to motor vehicle loans. Low- and moderate-income applicants are individuals who earn less than 80 percent of the median family income. In reviewing the information on low- and moderate-income applicants, the analysis relies upon the income reported by the applicant and used by the institution in making the credit decision. Income not reported or not relied upon in making the decision should not be included. Therefore, an applicant could earn more than 80 percent of the median family income, but be classified as low- and moderate-income based upon the reported income. Similar to the types of errors made by many financial institutions in HMDA loan application register reporting, many financial institutions, through inadvertent mistakes, could easily extract the figures from the loan application, and not the figures used in the underwriting decision, to report the gross annual income of the borrower.

At its option, an institution may provide other information to its federal financial supervisory agency concerning lending performance, including additional loan distribution data. Additional data might include loan commitments and loans outstanding.

If an institution elects to have loans made by any affiliate considered, for purposes of the lending or community development test or an approved strategic plan, the institution must collect, maintain, and report for those loans all of the data noted above, as applicable. For home mortgage loans, such an institution must also be prepared to identify the loans reported under HMDA by the affiliate.

If an institution elects to have loans made by a consortium or third party considered, the data indicated for the aggregate number and amount of community development loans originated or purchased must be reported as to these loans.

Identification of geographies in the assessment area represents one last item in the data collection and reporting requirements. A bank or thrift must collect and report by March 1 each year a list of the geographies in each assessment area.

The shift to performance-based examinations should increase the reliance on quantified data to assess institutions' performance. Inaccurate data may lead to inappropriate conclusions about an institution's CRA performance. Different departments or functions within a financial institution should receive thorough training on the data collection requirements of the revised CRA regulations. Obviously, data entry staff should be trained on the specifics of entering data for loan originations and purchases so that such employees perform this task with optimal accuracy. The typical deficiencies of HMDA reporting (insufficiently trained clerks entering data with little review from senior management) should not become the typical pattern of CRA data reporting. Although for most institutions, loan officers will never be called on to input the required CRA data collection, lending personnel (those involved in both originations and loan servicing) should be knowledgeable about all aspects of the CRA data collection requirements in order to serve as another control mechanism on CRA data integrity.

The data collection and reporting requirements will produce many questions concerning the intricacies of accurate CRA data reporting. In recognition of this, the FFIEC has developed a CRA assistance line for data collection and reporting responsibilities. The FFIEC has developed a fax information line that allows an individual to receive documents over a fax machine by calling a phone number and following the recorded instructions. The FFIEC's "fax-on-demand" information number is (202) 872-7584. Other than the cost of the phone call, this service is free.

In the interagency examination procedures applicable to institutions that must collect and report data, the agencies have included steps that require examiners to test samples of loan files to verify the accuracy of data collected and/or reported by the institution. Only by looking at a sample of actual loan files and comparing the original information with the information collected and/or reported by the institution will examiners be able to identify data errors. If an agency finds that an institution has substantial and/or intentional misreporting of data, the agency will consider citing a violation of its CRA regulation to discourage a similar practice in the future. The agencies recognize that institutions' data collection efforts the first year may encounter difficulties that could result in incompleteness and inaccuracies. The agencies have indicated they do not expect to impose sanctions or require costly resubmissions if an institution makes a good faith effort to collect and report data the first year.[16]

Given that the data collection and reporting requirements of the revised CRA regulations represent a tremendous expansion of workload for affected institutions, it is instructive to consider accuracy in CRA data collection and reporting by reference to institutions' previous experience with HMDA data collection requirements. The FRB's policy on HMDA data accuracy merits consideration as that agency's policy on HMDA data accuracy may shape the establishment of standards for accuracy in CRA data collection and reporting.

Some of the federal financial supervisory agencies have previously acknowledged data quality problems with HMDA data and have taken steps to improve the accuracy of HMDA data. However, while examination guidelines include procedures to assess HMDA data accuracy, they do not address the quality of other kinds of data used to assess performance, like other lending data or financial statistics. Moreover, the federal financial supervisory agencies do not have a uniform policy on what actions should be taken against institutions with poor HMDA data quality, and they have not been consistent in the actions they have taken to date.

Bank management is primarily responsible for ensuring that data provided by the institution are accurate, and examiners are responsible for verifying data accuracy during examinations. Among the four regulators, the FRB has done the most detailed analysis of HMDA data quality, which should be instructive regarding future sanctions for inaccuracy in CRA data collection and reporting. According to a 1995 General Accounting Office (GAO) report entitled *Challenges Remain to Successfully Implement the CRA,* the Federal Reserve District Banks participated in a survey from March 1993 to February

1994 to determine the quality of HMDA data submitted by state member banks for the year 1992 by cross-checking each institution's HMDA Loan Application Register (LAR) with its 1992 HMDA data submission.[17] This survey confirmed the FRB's long-standing concerns about HMDA data accuracy during this time period. The GAO report reveals that the FRB required one out of every five banks to resubmit its HMDA data for 1992.[18] The most significant errors found in these examinations involved the loan applicant's reported income. Over half of all income-related errors were the result of banks reporting income figures from unverified application information. The other half consisted mostly of clerical errors. FRB staff indicated these high error rates are because, in most institutions, HMDA reporting is done by insufficiently trained clerks, with little review from more senior management.[19]

Some institutions with poor HMDA data quality have been required to resubmit their data, while others have been subject to no such requirements. The FRB generally requires state member banks with a 10 percent or greater error rate to resubmit their HMDA data.[20] Other federal financial supervisory agencies do not have a specific policy on when resubmissions would be required. The FRB's policy on HMDA data accuracy may shape the establishment of standards for accuracy in CRA data collection and reporting.

The FRB has developed rules of materiality or significance concerning acceptable HMDA accuracy levels. For those banks regulated by the FRB, which number approximately 900 nationwide, errors in excess of 5 percent of a bank's reported HMDA data measured on a linear basis for 10 key critical fields will trigger the need to refile the HMDA LAR. The four location-related critical fields are the MSA (the metropolitan statistical area), the state, the county, and census tract. Two other key critical fields for purposes of the FRB's threshold accuracy standards include race and sex. Income and loan amount errors, but in neither case including rounding errors, also constitute key critical fields for purposes of the 5 percent error rate test. Lastly, the application date and the action taken date are key critical fields.

FRB member banks would be asked to refile an HMDA LAR if the error rate for the 10 key critical fields noted above exceeded 5 percent. An FRB member bank would also be asked to refile if the error rate for general errors other than the key critical fields noted above exceeded 10 percent. Errors are not measured on a literal basis. Errors, for the purpose of both the 5 percent threshold and the 10 percent general threshold, are counted on a line-by-line basis. That is, multiple errors within the same line constitute only one error for purposes of the FRB's accuracy test. It should be noted that, relative to the borrower's income amount and the loan amount, rounding errors do not count as to the 5 percent threshold but do count toward the 10 percent general error threshold.

The OTS and the OCC do not statistically sample HMDA data, as does the FRB pursuant to the elaborate methodology previously noted. OTS and OCC examiners undertake a "top-down" approach to HMDA compliance, with the major emphasis on the quality of the institution's management process and procedures. On the other hand, examiners from the FRB and the FDIC do specifically examine for HMDA LAR accuracy on a general basis.

The agencies will annually prepare individual CRA Disclosure Statements for each reporting institution and aggregate disclosure statements for each MSA and the non-MSA portion of each state. The agencies will make both the individual and the aggregate disclosure available to the public at central depositories.

The aggregate disclosure statements will indicate, for each geography, the number and amount of small business and small farm loans originated or purchased by all reporting institutions, except that the agencies may adjust the form of the disclosure if necessary, because of special circumstances, to protect the privacy of a borrower or the competitive position of an institution.

The disclosure statements for the individual institution will be prepared on a state-by-state basis and will contain for each county (and each assessment area smaller than a county) with a population of 500,000 or fewer in which the institution reported a small business or small farm loan: (1) the number and amount of small business and small farm loans located in low-, moderate-, middle-, or upper-income census tracts or block numbering areas; (2) a list of each census tract or block numbering area in the county or assessment area grouped according to whether the geography is low-, moderate-, middle-, or upper income; (3) a list of each census tract or block numbering area in which the institution reported a small business or small farm loan; and (4) the number and amount of small business and small farm loans to businesses and farms with gross annual revenues of $1 million or less. For each county (and each assessment area smaller than a county) with a population greater than 500,000, the number and amount of small business and small farm loans will be provided for geographies grouped according to whether the median income of the geography relative to the area median income is less than 10 percent, 10 or more but less than 20 percent, 20 or more but less than 30 percent, 30 or more but less than 40 percent, 40 or more but less than 50 percent, 50 or more but less than 60 percent, 60 or more but less than 70 percent, 70 or more but less than 80 percent, 80 or more but less than 90 percent, 90 or more but less than 100 percent, 100 or more but less than 110 percent, 110 or more but less than 120 percent, or 120 percent or more.

The disclosure statements will also contain information on the number and amount of loans inside each and outside any assessment area of the institution and the institution's community development loan information. The disclosure statements will include affiliate lending if the institution reported the affiliate lending for consideration in the institution's assessment.

In a theme repeated often in this book, the institution that has the best grasp of its performance context and that is most able to communicate that performance context to its federal financial supervisory agency will probably be the one judged as having the best results. Just as some institutions have in the past studied their own HMDA loan application registers, as well as those of "competitor" financial institutions, over time those institutions with the best CRA performance evaluations will also be those that studied carefully the annual individual CRA disclosure statements for each reporting institution and aggregate disclosure statements for each MSA. Institutions that have carefully studied individual CRA disclosure statements and aggregate disclosures for each MSA will be able to shape examiner perceptions of the small business and small farm lending opportunities within that assessment area. The increase in sophistication of loan distribution analysis that the financial institution industry has experienced over the last several years in the arena of home mortgage lending will be repeated in the context of small business and small farm lending through careful study of the information available in individual CRA disclosure statements and aggregate disclosure statements for each MSA.

Several thoughts on compliance design for an institution's data collection and data reporting responsibilities are in order. If one assumes that the data collection and reporting responsibilities of the CRA regulations will be handled in a fashion similar to HMDA reporting responsibilities, at too many financial institutions lenders generally have little responsibility for the accuracy and completeness of the HMDA LAR (loan application register) data. Although this would be a significant departure from the practice of many, if not most, financial institutions, a financial institution should make a senior lending manager ultimately responsible for the accuracy of data collected and reported under the CRA regulations and should give an assigned responsibility to a compliance officer only for advising, training, and monitoring. Data collection and reporting entries should be to lenders what a Bank Secrecy Act Currency Transaction Report (CTR) is to a teller—part and parcel of the job that must be done correctly or there are direct, adverse consequences. To make the compliance officer responsible for data accuracy is to assign responsibility for matters that he or she cannot control. Granted the number of data collection/reporting entries is far in excess of the number of Bank Secrecy Act CTRs filed by tellers, there is nonetheless tremendous merit to making operations personnel who work with a particular product personally responsible for the accuracy and completeness of required regulatory reports produced by the lending function.

[6] CRA PUBLIC FILE AND NOTICE

Under the revised CRA regulations effective July 1, 1995, the content and availability of the public file are more expansive than under the previous CRA regulations. The files must contain the following information:

1. All written comments received from the public for the current year and each of the prior two calendar years that specifically relate to the institution's performance in helping to meet community credit needs, and any response to the comments by the institution, if neither the comments nor the responses contain statements that reflect adversely on the good name or reputation of any persons other than the institution or publication of which would violate specific provisions of law.

2. A copy of the public section of the bank's most recent CRA performance evaluation prepared by the institution's federal financial supervisory agency.

3. A list of the bank's branches, their street addresses, and geographies.

4. A list of branches opened or closed by the bank during the current year and each of the prior two calendar years, their street addresses, and geographies.

5. A list of services (including hours of operation, available loan and deposit products, and transaction fees) generally offered at the bank's branches and descriptions of material differences in the availability or cost of services at particular branches, if any. At its option, an institution may include information regarding the availability of alternative systems for delivering retail banking services (e.g., remote service facilities not owned or operated by or exclusively for the bank, banking by telephone or computer, loan production offices, and bank-at-work or bank-by-mail programs).

6. A map of each assessment area showing the boundaries of the area and identifying the geographies contained within the area, either on the map or in a separate list.

7. Any other information that the bank chooses.

Relative to the first item in the above list (the bank's public file of written comments), most financial institutions routinely include far more information to respond to this item than is necessary. Bankers should realize that only written comments received from the public for the current year and each of the prior two calendar years that *specifically relate* to the institution's performance in helping to meet community credit needs must be placed in this file. Therefore, for example, a request for the bank's CRA statement does not meet this standard and should not be placed in this file. Similarly, thank-you letters acknowledging a gift to the local YMCA also do not meet this standard. Lastly, many financial institutions do not focus carefully on the time period in question. Some financial institutions have public file comment letters dating from the beginning of the CRA. A careful review of the contents of written comments probably would suggest for most, if not virtually all, financial institutions that there is nothing to place in the public file insofar as receipt of written comments are concerned that *specifically relate* to the institution's performance in helping to meet community credit needs.

On a related note, financial institutions are reminded to take advantage of one of the few remaining process-oriented opportunities in the evaluation regime contemplated by the revised CRA regulations. In that regard, financial institutions are encouraged to have friends of the institution write public file comment letters that extol the institution's performance in helping to meet community credit needs. Such a sample public file comment letter appears as Appendix 2.

For other than a small bank or a bank that was a small bank during the prior calendar year, the institution must include in its public file the following information pertaining to the institution and its affiliates, if applicable, for each of the prior two calendar years:

1. If the institution has elected to have one or more categories of the institution's consumer loans considered under the lending test, for each of these categories, the number and amount of loans
   a. to low-, moderate-, middle-, and upper-income individuals.
   b. located in low-, moderate-, middle-, and upper-income census tracts.
   c. located inside the institution's assessment area(s) and outside the institution's assessment area(s).

2. The bank CRA disclosure statement prepared by the institution's federal supervisory agency.

A bank or thrift required to report home mortgage loan data pursuant to HMDA Regulation C must include in the public file a copy of the HMDA disclosure statement provided by the Federal Financial Institutions Examination Council pertaining to the institution for each of the prior two calendar years. In addition, an institution that elected to have its federal supervisory agency consider the mortgage lending of an affiliate for any of these years must include in the institution's public file the affiliate's HMDA disclosure statement for those years. The institution must place the statement(s) in the public file within three business days after receipt.

A small bank or a bank that was a small bank during the prior calendar year must include in the public file the bank's loan-to-deposit ratio for each quarter of the prior calendar year and, at the institution's option, additional data on the institution's loan-to-deposit ratio; and the information concerning commercial and residential mortgage loan data if the institution has elected to be evaluated under the lending, investment, and service tests in lieu of the streamlined examination procedures otherwise available to small banks.

A bank or thrift that has been approved to be assessed under a strategic plan must include in the public file a copy of that plan. The institution need not include information submitted to the federal financial supervisory agency on a confidential basis in conjunction with the plan.

Any bank or thrift that received a less than satisfactory rating during the institution's most recent examination must include in the public file a description of the institution's current efforts to improve performance in helping to meet the credit needs of the institution's entire community. The institution is required to update the description quarterly. This requirement resembles in many ways the CRA statement required to be maintained under the old rules. For institutions subject to this requirement, an appropriate point of reference would be to have an outline of the institution's efforts that responds to the appropriate performance standard, that is, the lending, investment, and service test criteria for large banks, the small bank performance standards, possibly a strategic plan, and the community development test for limited purpose and wholesale institutions.

Under the revised CRA regulations effective July 1, 1995, access to the institution's CRA public file is broader than under the previous regulatory regime. A bank or thrift must make available to the public for inspection upon request and at no cost the following information: (1) at the main office and, if an inter-state institution, at one branch office in each state, all informa-tion in the public file; (2) at each branch, a copy of the public sec-tion of the institution's most recent CRA performance evaluation and a list of services provided by the branch; and (3) within five calendar days of the request, all the information in the public file relating to the assessment area in which the branch is located.

Under the revised CRA regulations, a bank or thrift should provide copies to a member of the public upon request, either on paper or in another form acceptable to the person making the request, of the information in the institution's public file. The institution may charge a reasonable fee not to exceed the cost of copying and mailing (if applicable).

An institution is generally required to ensure that the information required to be in the public file is current as of April 1 of each year.

The expanded content and availability access of an institu-tion's CRA public file make this topic especially suitable for employee training. Telephone receptionists and branch person-nel should be instructed where to transfer CRA-related inquiries, and should know the location and contents of the institution's public file.

Under the revised CRA regulations, public notice require-ments are similar to those currently in effect. A bank should post the "Community Reinvestment Act Notice" in the lobby of the main office and each of the institution's branches, as pro-vided in Section .44 of the CRA regulation of each of the federal financial supervisory agencies. The notice should be placed in an easily seen location, and should be sufficiently large to be read at a normal distance.

There are two different forms of CRA notice. Appendix B to the CRA regulation of each federal financial supervisory agency contains a notice that is used for main offices, and, if the institution is an interstate institution, one branch office in each state. There is additional language in this form of CRA notice concerning the fact that the appropriate federal financial supervisory agency publishes a nationwide list of the institutions that are scheduled for CRA examinations at least 30 days before the beginning of each quarter. That language does not appear in the form of CRA notice for branch offices. Furthermore, for financial institutions that are subsidiaries of a holding company, such institutions are required to include an additional two sentences as the last sentences appearing in the form of CRA notice appropriate for that type of institution. The additional language alerts the reader that the institution in question is an affiliate of a holding company (either a bank or savings and loan holding company). The reader is further advised by the language in the CRA notice to contact the regional director of the appropriate federal financial supervisory agency to request an announcement of applications covered by the CRA filed by holding companies. The form of notice for branch offices is simpler.

The new public file requirements will surprise many bank and thrift executives with unforeseen violations. The list of services (including hours of operation, available loan and deposit products, and transaction fees) that must be set forth in the public file represents a compliance trap for the unwary. As to consumer loans, home mortgage loans, and consumer deposit products, existing consumer protection laws such as the Truth in Lending Act, the Real Estate Settlement Procedures Act, the Expedited Funds Availability Act, the Truth in Savings Act, and the Electronic Funds Transfer Act provide a road map concerning transaction fees as to those particular products. There is, however, no regulatorily imposed road map provided for commercial lending insofar as disclosure of transaction fees is concerned. Because the notion of what constitutes transaction fees has no ready application in commercial lending, particular attention should be paid to the description of transaction fees that apply to commercial loans. Commercial deposit products likewise are not generally subject to the aforementioned consumer protection laws. Therefore, personnel who deal with deposit-side operations should think carefully about the "transaction fees" that can be applied to commercial deposit products. In addition, for banks whose franchise is geared toward serving the owner-operated small business community, there are many creative and unique accommodations offered for the commercial deposit accounts of such businesses. Deposit-side personnel should think carefully to make certain that all transaction fees and commercial deposit products are identified.

Because the information required by the public file availability obligation cuts across both deposit-side and loan-side operations, bank and thrift institutions should make certain that either the compliance officer or personnel intimately familiar with loan-related disclosure obligations (e.g., truth in lending, RESPA) and deposit-related disclosure obligations (e.g., truth in savings, expedited funds availability, and electronic funds transfer) oversee compliance with this obligation. The examination procedures indicate examiners will not review each branch for compliance with public file requirements.

It is instructive to consider the supervisory and examination experience of the FDIC, the federal financial supervisory agency regulating the largest number of financial institutions in the country. In the 12 months ending June 30, 1994, the FDIC reportedly examined more than 2,800 financial institutions for CRA compliance. Of those banks, more than 1,000 had committed CRA infractions. According to the FDIC survey released on July 8, 1994, the top 10 CRA violations listed in order of frequency were as follows:

- Failure to use prescribed language in the lobby poster.
- Inadequate maintenance of the CRA public files.
- Inadequate board of directors' review of the CRA program.
- Unreasonable delineation of communities made by banks.
- Failure to include the CRA notice in the CRA statement.
- Inadequate, incomplete, or inaccurate list of credit types that the bank is prepared to extend to its local community as set forth in the CRA statement.
- Failure to post the CRA notice in the public lobby of each bank office.

- Failure to use a map to portray the community delineation(s).
- Failure of the CRA statement to include a delineation of the local community.
- Failure to maintain each CRA statement for public inspection.[21]

While the cited top 10 CRA violations relate to the previous version of the CRA regulations in effect from 1978–1995, five of those violations will remain as requirements under the revised CRA regulations. With experience as a guide, bankers are instructed to pay special attention to public file and notice requirements.

Another compliance tip pertains to financial institutions involved in merger and acquisition activity. Following expansion via branch purchase or financial institution mergers, one should not neglect lobby signage and public notice requirements. In many cases, a financial institution involved in an acquisition or merger changes federal financial supervisory agency, possibly the name of the institution itself, phone numbers, and addresses. For financial institutions with numerous branches, making sure that the CRA notice and public file are accurate in all branches is a larger task than is commonly appreciated. Particularly in light of the expanded public file requirements, institutions have the potential for an even greater number of inadvertent CRA violations under the revised CRA regulations than they did under the previous version which served as the basis for the FDIC's survey concerning the 10 most frequently cited CRA violations.

NOTES

1. The National Technical Information Service (NTIS) is a bureau within the U.S. Department of Commerce that offers public access to thousands of government documents. To determine MSA boundaries, an institution may need to obtain FIPS PUB 8-5, *Metropolitan Statistical Areas,* from the NTIS, U.S. Department of Commerce, 5285 Port Royal Road, Springfield, VA 22161 (phone: 703-487-4650). NTIS

has also developed FedWorld, an on-line information system providing centralized public electronic access to federal government information resources. To access FedWorld by modem, dial (703) 321-3339 or telnet to FedWorld.gov; or file transfer protocol to ftp.FedWorld.gov; or on the WorldWide Web, point your browser to http://www.fedworld.gov.

2. Interagency Questions and Answers Regarding C.R.A., Federal Financial Institutions Examination Council, 58 Fed. Reg. 9176 (1993), Question 5.

3. 58 Fed. Reg. 67467, December 21, 1993.

4. 60 Fed. Reg. 22,156, 22,167 (May 4, 1995).

5. Id.

6. See an interagency document prepared by the OCC, the FDIC, the FRB, and the OTS entitled *Questions and Answers on CRA Data Collecting and Reporting,* question 9. For FDIC-supervised institutions, the document was provided as FIL-4-96, dated January 22, 1996.

7. Id.

8. Id.

9. Id.

10. Id.

11. Id.

12. Id.

13. Id., question 4.

14. Id.

15. Id.

16. See a letter, dated January 3, 1996, issued by the OCC, the FDIC, the FRB, and the OTS to Congressmen Henry B. Gonzalez, Bruce F. Vento, and Joseph P. Kennedy II, question and answer 5.b.

17. General Accounting Office Report GAO/GGD-96-23, *Community Reinvestment Act: Challenges Remain to Successfully Implement CRA,* November 1995, p. 60.

18. Id.

19. Id.

20. Id.

21. *ABA Bank Compliance, Regulatory & Legislative Advisory* (July 1994), Vol. XV, No. 7, at 2.

Strategic Plan Option

Institutions of any size may choose to have their CRA performance evaluated under the strategic plan option. Prerequisites to the strategic plan evaluation option include that the bank or thrift has submitted the plan to the institution's federal financial supervisory agency as provided in Section .27 of the CRA regulation of the agency; the agency has approved the plan; the plan is in effect; and the institution has been operating under an approved plan for at least one year. A CRA strategic plan may not exceed five years in duration, may address single or multiple assessment areas, and may include some or all appropriate affiliates. The CRA examination procedures make clear that an institution may develop a strategic plan for some but not all of the assessment areas that the institution serves.

Public participation is required in two phases: informally while developing the plan and formally for a 30-day comment period. An institution must solicit formal public comment by publishing a notice in "at least one newspaper of general circulation in each assessment area covered by the plan." Additionally, during the 30-day period, an institution availing itself of the strategic plan alternative must make copies of the plan available for review at all of the institution's offices in any assessment area covered by the plan.

The public participation provisions of the CRA regulation have been misunderstood by many bankers who think that the regulations give community organizations an inappropriate role in an institution's operations. The purpose of the consultation and community involvement requirements of the strategic plan evaluation option is for the institution to develop the fullest possible information about the needs of the institution's community and how those needs might be met. Nevertheless, the institution makes all decisions regarding how the institution plans to help meet those needs. It is important to note that in reviewing the public participation, the agencies will not consider whether community organizations unanimously support the plan, but whether the institution made appropriate investigation to determine the needs of the institution's community, and whether the goals of the plan serve those needs.[1]

A bank or thrift availing itself of the strategic plan alternative must submit the institution's plan to the institution's federal financial supervisory agency at least three months prior to the proposed effective date of the plan. An institution requesting approval for a strategic plan will generally need to submit the following to the institution's regulatory agency:

1. The names of each institution joining in the plan and a description of how they are affiliated. The agencies will approve a joint plan only if the plan provides measurable goals for each institution.
2. For each institution, an identification of the assessment area(s) covered by the plan, including a list of the geographies involved.
3. The proposed term of the plan. A plan may have a term of no more than five years.
4. The proposed effective date for the plan, which should be at least 90 days after the plan is submitted to the federal financial supervisory agency.
5. A description of the formal or informal public input received during development of the plan. Copies of any written comments that were received during the development of the plan may be provided.
6. A copy of the required public notice and the name(s) of the newspaper(s) in which the notice was published.

7. Copies of all written comments received during the comment period.

8. A copy of the strategic plan released for public comment if such a plan is different from the strategic plan being submitted for agency approval.

9. For each assessment area for each institution covered by the plan, copies of any information developed in the institution's normal business planning that the institution wants the federal financial supervisory agency to consider regarding lending, investment, and service opportunities in the assessment area, including a description of any legal constraints or limitations that affect the types of loans, investments, or services that the institution may make or offer.

10. For each assessment area for each institution covered by the plan, measurable goals for helping to meet the credit needs of the assessment area, particularly the needs of low- and moderate-income geographies and individuals. If the plan for an institution encompasses the activities of nondepository institution affiliates, the interagency guidelines for requesting approval for a strategic plan indicate it is not necessary to state separate goals for each such affiliate.

11. An indication whether any institution covered by the plan elects to be evaluated under another assessment method (e.g., large retail institution assessment method) if the institution fails to meet substantially the strategic plan goals for a satisfactory rating.

A bank must specify in its plan measurable goals for helping to meet the credit needs of each assessment area covered by the plan, particularly the needs of low- and moderate-income geographies and low- and moderate-income individuals, through lending, investment, and services, as appropriate. Review of several proposed strategic plans submitted to the FDIC during the first quarter of 1996 suggests that regulators will carefully review an institution's lending goals articulated toward low- and moderate-income areas and individuals. An institution's measurable goals should be most detailed with respect to the needs of low- and moderate-income geographies and low- and moderate-income individuals. As reported by the *American Banker,* at the National Compliance Conference of the American Bankers' Association held in early June 1996, a general concern that regulators have with the small number of proposed CRA strategic plans submitted through the beginning of June 1996 is the lack of specificity for lending goals.[2] For the few proposed CRA strategic plans that have been submitted, the federal financial supervisory agencies have been engaged in a back-and-forth parrying exercise in which the regulators request the submission of precise numbers concerning proposed lending goals.

Unless the bank has been designated as a wholesale or limited purpose bank, the bank's plan must emphasize lending and lending-related activities. The plan must specify measurable annual goals that constitute "satisfactory" performance, and multiyear plans must include annual interim measurable goals. A plan may specify measurable goals that constitute an "outstanding" performance. An institution may elect in its strategic plan that if the institution substantially fails to meet the plan goals for a satisfactory rating, the institution's CRA performance will be evaluated under (1) the lending, investment, and service tests; (2) the community development test; or (3) the small-institution performance standards, whichever may be appropriate. If such an election is not made in the strategic plan, the institution will be evaluated only under the strategic plan, and failure to meet the goals set forth for satisfactory performance will result in assignment of a rating of "needs to improve" or "substantial noncompliance."

Measurable goals are those stated in quantifiable terms. Institutions are provided flexibility in specifying goals. For example, an institution could provide ranges of lending amounts in different categories of loans. It would also be appropriate for an institution to plan on making a certain number of loans for lending a specific amount in a particular area or with respect to a particular project. Relative to community development services, an institution might plan on providing community services measured in terms of the frequency of use or amount of staff resources involved. According to the Interagency Guidelines for Requesting Approval for a Strategic Plan under the CRA, measurable goals may also be linked to funding requirements of certain public programs or indexed to other external factors as long as these mechanisms provide a quantifiable standard.

Review of proposed strategic plans submitted to the FDIC suggest that federal financial supervisory agencies will review carefully an institution's description of the formal or informal public input received during development of the plan. Institutions operating in urban areas should be prepared to provide a detailed explanation of how community groups are selected and how they are representative of low- and moderate-income areas in the institution's assessment area. Application processing for strategic plans reveals that the regulators have gone to some lengths to request any written comments received from these groups. Just as institutions are encouraged to have friendly public file comment letters that extol an institution's performance, institutions should also take advantage of the process-oriented aspect of the strategic plan alternative to have community groups provide written comments. Obviously not all community organization written comments will be welcomed by a financial institution, but to the extent that a financial institution can obtain a "positive" or "friendly" public written comment related to the institution's strategic plan, such items can shape a favorable regulatory perception of an institution's solicitation of public input during development of a strategic plan.

Information responsive to the institution's performance context is also critical in the submission of a strategic plan. Because a proposed strategic plan is evaluated by reference to the institution's performance context, institutions seeking to benefit from the strategic plan option must be particularly thorough in developing information regarding lending, investment, and service opportunities in the institution's assessment area. Regulators will require the information discussed in the second section (Performance Context) of Chapter 5. Unless an institution has developed information akin to that in a business plan, the institution is advised to gather this information before submitting the strategic plan. The failure to include this kind of information in the strategic plan application will only subject the institution to a request for additional information and delay the processing of the proposed strategic plan.

A bank may submit additional information to its federal financial supervisory agency on a confidential basis, but the goals stated in the plan must be sufficiently specific to enable the public and the federal financial supervisory agency to judge the merits of the plan.

The federal financial supervisory agency evaluates a plan's measurable goals using the following criteria, as appropriate:

1. The extent and breadth of lending or lending-related activities including, as appropriate, the distribution of loans among different geographies, businesses, and farms of different sizes, and individuals of different income levels; the extent of community development lending; and the use of innovative or flexible lending practices to address credit needs.

2. The amount and innovativeness, complexity, and responsiveness of the bank's qualified investments.

3. The availability and effectiveness of the bank's systems for delivering retail banking services and the extent and innovativeness of the bank's community development services.

A proposed strategic plan will be evaluated in the context of the information described in the performance context of the appropriate CRA regulation. This information could include, as appropriate, the following: demographic data on median income and household income; housing costs; lending, invest-ment, and service opportunities in the institution's assessment area(s); the institution's product offerings and business strat-egy; institutional capacity and constraints (including the insti-tution's size and financial condition and economic climate); past performance of the institution; and relevant information from the institution's public file. The agencies will not expect the institution to supply more information regarding the per-formance context than the institution would normally develop to prepare a business plan or to identify potential customers, including low- and moderate-income individuals or geographies in the institution's assessment area(s). Information submitted by the institution will be considered along with information from community, government, civic, and other sources.

According to the Interagency Guidelines for Requesting Approval for a Strategic Plan under the CRA, the proposed effective date of a strategic plan approval request should be at least 90 days after the request is submitted to the institution's federal financial supervisory agency. An agency will act upon an institution's request for approval of the institution's proposed strategic plan within 60 calendar days after the agency receives the complete plan, unless the agency extends the review period for good cause. The interagency guidelines for requesting approval of a CRA strategic plan provide that if the agency fails to act within the time period, the proposed plan will be deemed approved.

While many institutions are aware of the option to request confidential treatment of portions of the strategic plan, institutions should not overlook that under the provisions of the Freedom of Information Act, 5 U.S.C. 552, a request for approval of a proposed strategic plan submitted to the institution's federal financial supervisory agency is a public document and, as such, is available to the public on request. The agency's decision approving or denying a proposed strategic plan could also be available to the public under the Freedom of Information Act.

An institution may request confidential treatment for information that would be exempt from public disclosure under the Freedom of Information Act. For example, if the requesting institution is of the opinion that disclosure of commercial or financial information would likely result in substantial harm to the requesting institution's competitive position or that of the institution's affiliates, or that disclosure of information of a personal nature would result in a clearly unwarranted invasion of personal privacy, confidential treatment of such information may be requested. This request for confidential treatment must be submitted in writing concurrently with the filing of the strategic plan and must discuss in detail the justification for confidential treatment. Justification must be provided for each item or category of information for which confidential treatment is requested. The institution's request for confidentiality should explain the harm that would result from public release of the information.

Under the processing standards for requesting confidential treatment, an institution should segregate from the other information that is submitted that information for which confidential treatment is sought, specifically identify the nonconfidential portion of the strategic plan and the confidential section, and label as "confidential" information for which confidential treatment is sought. The same procedure would apply to any institution requesting confidentiality with regard to the filing of supplemental information.

During the term of the plan, a bank or thrift may request that the institution's federal financial supervisory agency approve an amendment to the plan on grounds that there has been a material change in circumstances. Any amendment requires compliance with the two-stage public comment process previously described.

The conventional wisdom proffered by regulators and industry commentators is that large institutions, those with nontraditional business strategies, and affiliated institutions might logically be expected to use the strategic plan alternative. For those institutions that would undertake extensive efforts to ascertain community credit needs, distill those observations into a coherent plan and set of goals, communicate the plan and goals to the appropriate persons within the organization, monitor execution of the CRA plan, and make appropriate corrections as interim results warrant, the work necessary to achieve outstanding CRA results systematically should be largely the same, whether under the strategic plan alternative or the performance standards normally applicable to that type of institution.

The adage "pay me now or pay me later" rings particularly true in the decision whether to pursue the strategic plan option. While the initial cost to develop a strategic plan will be high in terms of employee time, financial investment, and possible consultant expertise, the outcome is most attractive of all the standards for CRA performance evaluation. All other methods of CRA performance evaluation depend largely on examiner perceptions. With the strategic plan option, the financial institution can establish measurable goals which make the CRA examination procedure predictable and therefore remove the subjective analysis of examiners. Granted there is considerable start-up cost associated with the development of a strategic plan and thereafter with costs associated with monitoring the plan to make certain the institution is in compliance with the plan's measurable goals, the back-end costs at the time of evaluation are minimal. This would be the exact opposite result for most financial institutions that respond to events and examiner perceptions, rather than actively shaping the regulatory assessment process. Responding to the regulatory assessment process takes time, whether in the normal ad hoc fashion of financial institutions in responding to regulators or in crafting a coherent plan through the strategic plan alternative. When one considers what damage control can entail both in terms of time commitment and expense, the idea of committing resources to a strategic plan recommends itself because the attainment of satisfactory results is far more likely.

Banks should also carefully assess the potential impact of public participation in development of the strategic plan. For many, if not most, financial institutions in the country, bankers' closet fears that community organizations represent "rabid socialists" are probably misplaced. Community organizations, as a general rule, tend to be most active in large urban areas, particularly on both the East Coast and West Coast, and are strikingly less active in many small towns and rural markets. Notwithstanding the hype that the public participation provisions of the CRA regulations provide community organizations with an inappropriate role in an institution's operations, many financial institutions making use of the strategic plan alternative will be pleasantly surprised to discover that the much-feared opportunity for public comment turns out to be a non-event in terms of substance. In many markets, there may not even be any community organizations. Thus, when one recognizes that the revised CRA regulations represent a tremendous expansion of workload and that costs of related CRA compliance have increased significantly, the decision is essentially whether to bear those costs up front in the form of the strategic plan alternative or to bear them at the back end in the all too typical form of last-minute planning for CRA exams.

If an institution chooses the strategic plan alternative, the institution's federal financial supervisory agency will consider the institution's actual performance compared to the plan's stated goals. According to the Interagency Guidelines for Requesting Approval for a Strategic Plan under the CRA, examiners will consider the extent and degree to which goals were met, the relative importance of unmet goals, the impact of unmet goals on low- and moderate-income persons and geographies, and the reasons for unmet goals. Given that strategic plans by their nature are fairly unique to each institution, the examiner may of necessity have to ask the institution for the data to determine whether the institution has met the plan goals.

If the institution substantially achieves the plan goals for a satisfactory rating, the appropriate federal financial supervisory agency will rate the institution's performance under the plan as "satisfactory." If the institution exceeds the plan goals for a satisfactory rating and substantially achieves the plan goals for an outstanding rating, the appropriate federal financial supervisory agency will rate the institution's performance under the plan as "outstanding." If the institution substantially fails to meet the plan goals for a satisfactory rating, the appropriate federal financial supervisory agency will rate the institution as either "needs to improve" or "substantial noncompliance," depending on the extent to which the institution falls short of the plan goals, unless the institution elected in its plan to be rated otherwise, under (1) the lending, investment, and service tests, (2) the community development test, or (3) the small institution performance standards, whichever may be appropriate.

NOTES

1. 60 Fed. Reg. 22,156, 22,169 (May 4, 1995).
2. "Regulators: CRA Strategic Plans Fall Short in Numbers, Detail," *American Banker,* June 6, 1996, p. 11.

CHAPTER 7

Regulatory Assessment for Limited Purpose and Wholesale Institutions

Wholesale or limited purpose banks are evaluated under a separate CRA performance standard, referred to as the community development test. This standard assesses a wholesale or limited purpose bank's record of making qualified investments, engaging in community development lending, and providing community development services. The regulatory assessment for limited purpose and wholesale institutions recognizes that these institutions are not engaged in traditional retail lending activities.

A wholesale or limited purpose bank may be assessed under the separate CRA standard for this category of institution, provided that the wholesale or limited purpose bank requests such a designation at least three months prior to the proposed effective date of the designation, and the institution is designated as a wholesale or limited purpose bank by the institution's federal financial supervisory agency. Interagency guidelines for requesting designation as a wholesale or limited purpose institution indicate that a request for designation as a wholesale or limited purpose institution should state how the institution satisfies either the wholesale institution or limited purpose institution definition.

Absent a request for designation as a limited purpose or wholesale institution, an institution whose profile might otherwise suggest that the institution fits this niche would be evaluated under the strategic plan alternative, small bank assessment (assuming compliance with the asset size threshold), or large bank assessment.

The interagency guidelines for requesting designation as a wholesale or limited purpose institution provide that a so-called "niche institution" (an institution that is in the business of lending to the public, but that specializes in certain types of retail loans or extending credit to a group of borrowers with, for example, certain financial or professional characteristics) would not generally qualify as a wholesale or limited purpose institution. A savings association or savings bank would generally not qualify as a limited purpose institution absent additional limitations on the institution's activities.

The statement requesting designation as a limited purpose or wholesale institution should contain facts and data sufficient to describe the nature of the institution's current and prospective business, credit products offered, and the market area served. For a de novo institution, the interagency guidelines state that the written request must include a business plan that contains a description of the institution's proposed nature of business, credit and other product(s) to be offered, and the market area to be served.

If the institution engages in retail or other lending activities that may not be viewed as consistent with the institution's request for designation as a wholesale or limited purpose institution, the interagency guidelines state that the institution should provide sufficient information about those activities to allow the institution's federal financial supervisory agency to determine whether the activities are infrequent, incidental, or performed on an accommodation basis. This information should address the following elements, as appropriate:

1. Describe each type of activity and the conditions or circumstances under which the institution offers the product or service. (For example, if the institution engages in mortgage lending, explain whether such loans are offered to the general public, or, for example, are offered only to corporate customers or employees of the institution.)

2. State the percentage of the institution's assets and income that each activity represents.
3. Explain how the incidental lending activity relates to the institution's assessment area(s).
4. State whether the volume of incidental lending activity would be sufficient to allow for a reasonable evaluation of the institution's performance under the lending test.

The interagency guidelines for requesting designation as a wholesale or limited purpose institution also require a description of (a) any legal constraints or limitations that affect the type of credit services that the institution may offer and (b) the institution's assessment area(s) and the location of the institution's branches and offices. The institution's assessment area(s) must generally consist of one or more MSAs or one or more contiguous political subdivisions in which the institution has its main office, branches, and deposit-taking ATMs.

The institution's statement requesting designation as a limited purpose or wholesale institution must also explain how the institution's network of branches is consistent with the designation as a wholesale or limited purpose institution and state the proposed effective date for the designation, which should be at least 90 days after the request is submitted to the institution's federal financial supervisory agency.

According to the interagency guidelines, the federal financial supervisory agency will normally notify the institution in writing of the agency's decision to approve or deny the request within 60 days of receiving a complete written request. If approved, the designation remains in effect until the institution requests revocation of the designation or until one year after the federal financial supervisory agency notifies the institution that the federal financial supervisory agency has revoked the designation on the agency's own initiative.

Under the provisions of the Freedom of Information Act, a request for designation as a wholesale or limited purpose institution that is submitted to the institution's federal financial supervisory agency is a public document and is available to the public upon request. The federal financial supervisory agency's decision approving or denying a request for designation may also be available to the public under the Freedom of Information Act.

An institution may request confidential treatment for information that would be exempt from the disclosure requirements of the Freedom of Information Act. If the requesting institution is of the opinion that disclosure of commercial or financial information would be likely to result in substantial harm to the requesting institution's competitive position or that of the institution's affiliates, or that disclosure of information of a personal nature would result in a clearly unwarranted invasion of personal privacy, confidential treatment of such information may be requested. This request for confidential treatment must be submitted in writing concurrently with the filing of the request for designation as a wholesale or limited purpose institution and must discuss in detail the justification for confidential treatment. Justification must be provided for each category of information for which confidential treatment is requested. The institution's request for confidentiality should explain the harm that would result from public release of this information.

According to the interagency guidelines for requesting designation as a limited purpose or wholesale institution, information for which confidential treatment is sought should be (1) segregated from the other information that is submitted; (2) specifically identified in the nonconfidential portion of the designation request (by reference to the confidential section); and (3) labeled "Confidential." The requesting institution should follow this same procedure on confidentiality with regard to filing any supplemental information. The institution's federal financial supervisory agency will determine whether information labeled "Confidential" will be so regarded, and will advise the requesting institution of any decision to make information labeled "Confidential" available to the public.

According to the interagency guidelines for requesting designation as a limited purpose or wholesale institution, an institution should follow the rules stated above when submitting confidential supervisory information, which includes any information contained in, related to, or derived from reports of examination and inspection, or confidential operating and condition reports.

Regulators assess the CRA performance of a wholesale or limited purpose institution according to the following criteria:

1. The number and amount of community development loans, qualified investments, or community development services.
2. The use of innovative or complex qualified investments, community development loans, or community development services, and the extent to which the investments are routinely provided by private investors.
3. The bank's responsiveness to credit and community development needs.

At the institution's option, the federal financial supervisory agency will consider the institution's indirect activities, such as qualified investment or community development services provided by an affiliate of the institution and lending by affiliates, consortiums, and third parties.

All qualified investments, community development loans, and community development services must benefit the assessment area of the wholesale or limited purpose bank. A wholesale or limited purpose bank can include qualified investments, community development loans, and services outside such institution's assessment area, as long as the institution has adequately addressed the needs of its designated assessment area.

Wholesale and limited purpose banks are given some flexibility in calculating the number and amount of community development loans. For example, wholesale or limited purpose banks, in contrast to retail banks, may count community development loans wherever such loans are located, as long as the wholesale or limited purpose bank has otherwise adequately addressed the credit needs in the institution's assessment area. Additionally, wholesale and limited purpose banks may count any home mortgage loan, small business loan, small farm loan, and consumer loan as a community development loan. In calculating community development loans (as well as qualifying investments in community development services), a wholesale or limited purpose bank may count the loans, investments, and services of affiliates and a pro rata share of those made by third parties in which the wholesale or limited purpose bank has an interest.

Documentation

Much has been written and spoken to the effect that the revised CRA regulations represent a deliverance from the documentation requirements which came to characterize CRA compliance from 1989 through the present. While it is true that the federal financial supervisory agencies no longer will consider detailed documentation of every contact or credit ascertainment effort to demonstrate performance, the effect of the revised CRA regulations for other than institutions evaluated under the small bank performance standards represents a considerable expansion of documentation requirements. The kind of documentation necessary to show CRA compliance efforts has changed considerably under the revised CRA regulations.

In the summer of 1992, the FFIEC, in an effort to simplify and streamline compliance supervisory processes and pursue reduction in regulatory burden, issued guidance regarding record keeping and documentation under the CRA. This guidance emphasizes that the agencies base their evaluation of CRA performance primarily on how well an institution helps to meet the credit needs of its community or communities, not on the amount of documentation the institution generates or maintains. The interagency guidance also indicates that a lack of documentation is not a sufficient basis on which to issue a poor rating if an institution's performance can otherwise be determined to be satisfactory or better.

The documentation expected by the agencies is primarily that which is useful to the institution's own management needs. In a well-managed CRA program, a financial institution's board of directors and management use relevant documentation to make certain that their programs are working as planned. The regulatory agencies will use this documentation in their assessment of the institution's CRA performance and to make sure that a proper level of management oversight of the institution's CRA program is in place. Documents such as the minutes of the board of directors' meetings, program plans, marketing plans, advertising scripts, geographic analysis, and other information that the institution prepares and maintains for its own management use should demonstrate the level of CRA performance.

Even though the revised CRA regulations indicate that small institutions are not subject to any requirement to conduct formal loan distribution analysis, fair lending compliance and minimal CRA compliance suggest that if an institution's management does not know where the institution's loans are being originated, it is unlikely that the institution is carrying out its responsibilities under the CRA and the fair lending laws.

Loan distribution analysis requires a financial institution's management to have an understanding of the institution's loan distributions to minorities, in minority areas (particularly African-American areas), to low- and moderate-income borrowers and in low- and moderate-income areas. Now that the new CRA regulations codify and expand upon the FFIEC policy statement on loan distribution analysis, virtually all institutions will be exploring quantitative CRA documentation to a degree that they might not have done before, in order to determine (a) which segments of their assessment areas are low- and moderate-income and (b) the extent of the institution's loan penetration in those low- and moderate-income segments of the assessment areas, and in order to conduct various demographic and other analysis necessary to establish an appropriate performance context for the institution.

Loan distribution analysis has become an essential part not only of fair lending compliance, but of CRA compliance as well. Loan distribution analysis is necessary not only to determine whether an institution has been in compliance with the CRA and fair lending laws, but also to help an institution to direct its future compliance efforts. Loan distribution analysis should become an integral part of management deliberations concerning loan marketing and production, rather than being merely an after-the-fact responsibility of the CRA officer to quantify CRA and fair lending compliance. In this way, an institution can assure itself that it is exercising the greatest degree of control over its CRA and fair lending compliance and the outcome of its CRA performance assessment.

The clear lesson that has emerged from fair lending cases and CRA regulation over the past few years is that each and every bank and thrift must ensure (1) that the institution's banking products and services are made available and marketed with equal vigor to each and every sector of its community(ies); (2) that the institution undertakes as a *routine* part of its CRA compliance a careful analysis of its geographic loan distribution (particularly, but not exclusively, an analysis of its home mortgage loan distribution) to identify areas or income groups within its community that are underrepresented; (3) that a similar analysis is undertaken to ascertain whether minorities are underrepresented among its borrowers; and (4) if a pattern of disparate impact emerges from the analysis, that the institution (*a*) be able to account for (explain) why minorities are underrepresented relative to the expected loan distribution and (*b*) take immediate steps to correct the underrepresentation of minorities within its borrower base.

The analysis should be performed for each loan product, for each census tract within an assessment area, for each assessment area, and so on, and the analysis should focus on, among other things, distributions of loans to (1) low-income and moderate-income individuals and neighborhoods versus middle- and upper-income borrowers and (2) minority (particularly African-American) borrowers versus white borrowers. A sample format for loan distribution analysis appears in Appendix 1. A final point on the subject of loan distribution analysis is that loan distribution data represent only one-half of the equation.

The other half, knowing the demographics and demographic trends in the market(s) in which an institution operates, is at least as important. Without this information, loan distribution analysis can paint a deceptively bad picture, and the institution is deprived of information that would help the institution to customize its product offerings and marketing efforts in low- and moderate-income areas to greatest effect. Some census tracts can, for example, be so underprivileged that there is virtually no opportunity for lending to residents within such a tract, or they can have virtually no sales of residences within a particular time period, preventing any lenders from making home purchase loans in those tracts. Thus, one would like to know such demographic data as the number of owner-occupied housing units in a tract, the median age and value of the housing units, the average or actual number of home sale transactions within a year, the percentage of those that were financed, the percentage of the latter that were financed through mortgage brokers or with government-assistance in some form, and so on.

For most financial institutions in cities across the country, HMDA data show loan denial and acceptance rates for various races and income categories indicating that the institution has a disproportionately high denial rate for African-American applicants versus white applicants. This is a systemic problem. However, the significance of the disparity in white versus black loan denial rates cannot be dismissed. An institution that does not perform the necessary demographic and loan distribution analyses might be more vulnerable to criticism than the institution whose demographic and loan distribution analyses form a basis upon which that institution is able to explain, clarify, or correct an apparently high denial rate for African-Americans.

If a financial institution seeks to deal with its federal financial supervisory agency from a position of strength, documentation is necessary to reverse examiner perceptions or findings that may be based on erroneous, misinterpreted, or incomplete data. While CRA-related documentation would be expected to be less formal and less extensive in small institutions than in larger urban institutions, every financial institution should assemble a CRA documentation file with an individual file folder for each of the seven items noted in the performance context discussed in the second section of Chapter 5. In addition, the institution should have a file folder that addresses each item of the performance tests and standards applicable to that institution. Thus, if an institution is subject to evaluation under the lending, investment, and service tests, the institution would have a file folder with documentation responsive to each element under the lending, investment, and service tests. A wholesale or limited purpose institution would likewise have a file folder for each of the performance criteria for that category of institution. An institution subject to evaluation under the small bank performance standards would have a file folder for each of the five small bank performance criteria. Lastly, an institution subject to evaluation under the strategic plan would perhaps have the simplest documentation requirements. Only that documentation necessary to show compliance with the institution's strategic plan should be necessary. Evidence of an institution's CRA program and processes should be appropriately catalogued under the applicable factor in the comprehensive CRA documentation file maintained by the institution.

What is clearly no longer necessary under the revised CRA regulations are records relevant to CRA-related meetings, contacts, phone calls, and other outreach. In addition, officer call reports no longer recommend themselves.

Until several years' experience under the revised CRA regulations proves otherwise, another reason to continue documenting CRA compliance is that there must be value in being able to demonstrate that the institution tried to achieve outstanding CRA results, even if the institution's efforts were not entirely successful. Competitive standing and market share analysis is likely to be of greater import to large institutions than it will be to institutions subject to evaluation under the small bank performance standards. If market share analysis plays a large role in CRA performance evaluations, for many institutions, documentation will be all that the institution can show. For those institutions with a disproportionately small share of the low- and moderate-income lending market relative to an institution's overall market share, the absence of documentation leaves management ill-prepared to rebut examiner perceptions of CRA performance.

CHAPTER 9

Ratings

At the completion of each examination, the examining agency is required to prepare a written evaluation of the institution's CRA compliance record. This written evaluation includes the institution's record of meeting the credit needs of its entire community, particularly low- and moderate-income neighborhoods. The written evaluation is composed of a public section and a confidential section. The public section is made available for public inspection for the purpose of allowing the public to know both what the regulatory agencies are telling the institutions and what the CRA records of the particular institution are.

The public section:

1. States the examining agency's conclusions for each performance factor identified by each respective regulatory agency's CRA regulations.
2. Discusses the facts and data supporting such conclusions.
3. Contains the institution's rating for meeting community credit needs.

The four ratings that can be assigned to an institution are:

1. Outstanding record of meeting community credit needs.
2. Satisfactory record of meeting community credit needs.

3. Needs to improve record of meeting community credit needs.

4. Substantial noncompliance in meeting community credit needs.

The ratings have been made public for all evaluations conducted after July 1, 1990.

Although the CRA regulations provide no formal mechanism to contest the rating that an institution receives, some institutions have petitioned their regulatory agencies for a reevaluation of their rating. According to the July 3, 1991, *American Banker,* both Harris Trust and Savings Bank, Chicago, Illinois, and IBJ Schroder, New York, New York, requested reevaluations from their respective Federal Reserve Banks of Chicago and New York after receiving a "needs to improve" CRA rating. Since 1991, the federal financial supervisory agencies have developed formal appeals processes. While an appeal contesting a rating classification in 1991 would have been unlikely to be successful, the supervisory appeals system in place at each of the four federal financial supervisory agencies makes it possible that an institution's appeal of the institution's CRA rating could be successful.

The confidential section of the evaluation contains any references that identify any customer, employee, or officer of the institution, or any person or organization that has provided information in confidence to a federal or state financial supervisory agency, and any statements obtained or made by the regulatory agency in the course of an examination which in the judgment of the agency are too sensitive or speculative to disclose to the institution or to the public.

The confidential section may be disclosed, in whole or in part, to the institution if the appropriate federal financial supervisory agency determines that such disclosure will promote the objectives of the CRA. Nonetheless, such disclosure is not to identify a person or organization that provided information in confidence to a federal or state financial supervisory agency.

Approximately 90 percent of all institutions examined for CRA compliance have received a "satisfactory" rating or better since July 1990 when, as a result of amendments to CRA, ratings were made public, and the rating scale was changed.[1] Table 9–1, which was extracted from a 1995 General Accounting Office report to Congress, shows aggregate CRA ratings and ratings by each federal financial supervisory agency since July 1, 1990, when the regulators began publicly disclosing CRA ratings.[2]

Table 9–1 shows what the thrift industry knows only too well: the OTS is the toughest CRA grader. On the other hand, the FRB is the "easiest" CRA grader. Table 9–1 shows that enforcement consistency has been a problem in the CRA rating evaluation process. CRA scores provided through the first four months of 1996 again show that the OTS is the "toughest" CRA rating agency, and the FRB is the federal financial supervisory agency that hands out the smallest number and percentage of "needs to improve" and substantial noncompliance ratings. To borrow the famous French phrase, the more things change, the more they remain the same.

It seems unlikely that the regulators undertook more than two years of painstaking rulemaking procedures in order that 90 percent of institutions will continue to receive ratings of satisfactory or better. As a practical matter, it seems very likely that more institutions will receive ratings of "needs to improve" or worse. The institutions that are most vulnerable are those that (1) have a disproportionately small share of the low- and moderate-income lending market relative to the institutions' overall market shares and (2) have not undertaken a concerted effort to identify low- and moderate-income credit opportunities and to create and market special credit products for those markets. Although the proof for this assertion will not likely be available until after July 1, 1997, the date CRA performance evaluations are provided for large retail banks, market share analyses are likely to be regarded by examiners as one of the most probative indicators of CRA performance, if not the most important.

Another old proverb, "a stitch in time saves nine," has particular application to the revised CRA regulations. The point of the new CRA rules is to emphasize results over process; in application, however, "results" will mean market share. A brave new world is dawning in CRA compliance, and the upshot of CRA performance evaluations over the next several years will

T A B L E 9–1

CRA Ratings for All Banks and Thrifts Examined
from July 1, 1990, through December 31, 1994

	1990		1991	
Regulators & Rating	**Number**	**Percentage**	**Number**	**Percentage**
FRB				
Outstanding	35	11	75	11
Satisfactory	239	78	544	80
Needs to improve	30	10	52	8
Substantial noncompliance	4	1	5	1
Total	388	100	676	100
FDIC				
Outstanding	78	6	240	9
Satisfactory	1,093	83	2,286	83
Needs to improve	144	11	215	8
Substantial noncompliance	6	0	27	1
Total	1,321	100	2,768	100
OCC				
Outstanding	13	13	95	11
Satisfactory	73	71	674	76
Needs to improve	15	15	112	13
Substantial noncompliance	2	2	9	1
Total	103	100	890	100
OTS				
Outstanding	19	5	67	8
Satisfactory	255	72	594	74
Needs to improve	74	21	128	16
Substantial noncompliance	8	2	18	2
Total	356	100	807	100
All Regulators				
Outstanding	145	7	477	9
Satisfactory	1,660	80	4,098	80
Needs to improve	263	13	507	10
Substantial noncompliance	20	1	59	1
Total	2,088	100	5,141	100

1992		1993		1994	
Number	**Percentage**	**Number**	**Percentage**	**Number**	**Percentage**
80	13	127	20	123	22
493	78	491	75	430	76
49	8	27	4	9	2
7	1	6	1	3	1
629	100	651	100	565	100
452	14	529	14	587	17
2,668	81	2,939	81	2,638	77
165	5	168	5	182	5
15	0	14	0	7	0
3,300	100	3,650	100	3,414	100
89	11	193	15	192	20
614	77	988	77	736	76
93	12	99	8	37	4
2	0	2	0	3	0
798	100	1,282	100	968	100
90	10	162	15	105	16
667	74	827	76	515	77
141	16	90	8	46	7
5	0	3	0	1	0
903	100	1,082	100	667	100
711	13	1,011	15	1,007	18
4,442	79	5,245	79	4,319	77
448	8	384	6	274	5
29	1	25	0	14	0
5,630	100	6,665	100	5,614	100

Note: Ratings for the year 1990 include only those given by the regulators from July 1, 1990, the effective date of public disclosure of CRA ratings, to the end of the year.

be that many institutions (more than 10 percent), to their surprise and dismay, will receive the dreaded "needs to improve" moniker.

Retail institutions that are evaluated under the lending, investment, and service tests will be assigned a rating based upon the assigned rating principles and the matrix that implements these principles, with adjustment for any evidence of discrimination. The federal financial supervisory agencies have developed a matrix that sets forth the methodology for aggregating an institution's scores on the lending, service, and investment tests to arrive at an assigned rating. The number of points to be given for each rating on the lending, service, and investment tests appears in the following table:

Component Test Ratings	Lending	Service	Investment
Outstanding	12	6	6
High Satisfactory	9	4	4
Low Satisfactory	6	3	3
Needs to Improve	3	1	1
Substantial Noncompliance	0	0	0

To achieve each of the composite assigned ratings, the table below specifies the number of points needed to achieve that assigned rating.

Points	Composite Assigned Rating
20 or over	Outstanding
11 through 19	Satisfactory
5 through 10	Needs to Improve
0 through 4	Substantial Noncompliance

For institutions that are evaluated under the community development test for wholesale or limited purpose institutions, the small institution performance standards, or an approved strategic plan, ratings on these tests will be the institution's assigned rating with adjustment for any evidence of discrimination.

Evidence of discrimination will be considered in assigning a rating to all banks and thrifts, regardless of whether they are evaluated under the lending, service, and investment tests, the community development test for wholesale or limited purpose institutions, the smallest institution assessment method, or the strategic plan option. Evidence of lending discrimination is a "wild card" factor that adversely affects any institution's CRA rating. In determining the effect of discriminatory or other illegal credit practices on an institution's CRA rating, a federal financial supervisory agency would consider the nature and extent of the evidence, the policies and procedures that the institution has in place to prevent the discrimination or other illegal credit practices, and any corrective action that the institution has taken or has committed to take, particularly voluntary corrective action resulting from self-assessment and other relevant information such as the institution's past fair lending performance.

Bank and thrift institutions must conduct a delicate balancing act when they consider proactive measures to ameliorate the gap between loan approval rates to minorities versus nonminorities. As lenders seek greater penetration of minority and low- and moderate-income markets, African-American loan application denials often increase at a faster rate than the increase in applications both from minority areas and from minority applicants. As a financial institution increases in absolute terms the number of loans made to minorities, including African-Americans, to low- and moderate-income persons, and in minority and low- and moderate-income areas, the bank must remain attentive to loan denial rates and undertake to ensure that minorities are accorded the same consideration as nonminorities in the loan application process, the essence of the fair lending statutes.

Many financial institutions which rank among the largest residential mortgage lenders in their market receive examination comments, either directly or indirectly, that the institution must increase loan originations to African-Americans. To respond to these regulatory recommendations and to have a competitive market-share standing under the market share "beauty pageant" now employed by the federal financial supervisory agencies in CRA performance evaluations, many lenders consider offering a loan program with concessionary terms available solely to members of certain racial or ethnic groups.

Although conceived with noble intentions, offering a loan program with concessionary terms only to members of certain racial or ethnic groups can expose the lender to violation of the Fair Housing Act (FHA) and the Equal Credit Opportunity Act (ECOA). Both statutes provide for private recovery by individuals who have had their rights violated under these statutes and provide for class action recovery and attorneys' fees. A bank must consider this private liability exposure as the institution designs a loan program targeted to African-Americans.

Under the FHA and the ECOA, a bank may not base lending decisions on a prohibited basis, including on the basis of race. Therefore, a bank cannot grant preferential treatment to African-American applicants, just as it cannot grant such treatment to white applicants. If an institution wishes to increase loan originations to African-Americans, the better way would be to structure a loan program targeted exclusively to low- and moderate-income potential customers. Statistically, African-Americans do comprise a large share of the low- and moderate-income population within this country.

If a bank were to develop a loan program involving concessionary lending terms and target the program to low- and moderate-income residents, how the bank markets that product is another question. The bank can place special marketing emphasis within African-American communities or conduct outreach activities through realtors with a following in the communities, churches, and advertising sources that cater to the minority community. Most of the lenders who have signed consent decrees with the Justice Department involving alleged discrimination were required to develop a special marketing initiative with a "message" designed specifically for minority customer groups.

Lenders should not misunderstand the difference between their CRA obligations and fair lending requirements (FHA and ECOA). On July 18, 1994, Eugene Ludwig, the Comptroller of the Currency, stated that the nation's fair lending laws still lack clarity and certainty, despite efforts by regulators to refine their fair lending examination procedures and interpretations. Speaking at an FFIEC-sponsored fair lending seminar, Mr. Ludwig acknowledged that the statutes are "not yet clear enough to resolve many of the operational questions that banks--and bank regulators—face as we seek to make equal opportunity lending a reality in this country."[3] As reported in the *American Banker*, Mr. Ludwig noted that *"activities intended to provide equal economic opportunity could prove unlawful"* (emphasis added). He noted, "Credit counseling programs, flexible underwriting standards, and *special loan products targeted to specific population groups, could fail the test of equal treatment,* however desirable they might be by other policy lights" (emphasis added).[4]

Well-intentioned loan programs involving concessionary lending terms to specific population groups could be seen as violative of fair lending statutes. Such lending discrimination could negatively impact an institution's CRA performance evaluation. The very reason that lenders consider loan programs targeted to specific population groups (to remedy the gap between approval rates to nonminorities versus minorities) could, if poorly conceived in design and execution, subject an institution to a "needs to improve" CRA performance evaluation on the basis of lending discrimination.

An institution seeking to improve its market share in lending to targeted groups may wish to consider an innovative loan correspondent arrangement that recently became permissible under the Real Estate Settlement Procedures Act ("RESPA"). In the loan referral arrangement, a mortgage broker (or realtor or other correspondent) would (1) take a residential loan application on an application form supplied by the retail lender from a prospective home purchaser/customer of the real estate brokerage firm, (2) provide the enumerated services defined by the correspondent agreement between the mortgage broker firm and the retail lender and (3) receive a fee from the retail lender for the application-taking and loan processing services performed incident to the application and credit approval processes. While the mortgage broker would perform certain enumerated application-taking and loan processing services, the retail lender would originate, underwrite, close, and fund the mortgage-broker-initiated loans in the retail lender's own name, using employees and facilities of the retail lender.

The retail lender's intent should be to structure a correspondent arrangement with the mortgage broker such that the mortgage broker performs a mix of counseling and noncounseling services as identified in a February 14, 1995, letter from the Department of Housing and Urban Development ("HUD") that are compensable under HUD interpretive standards governing

RESPA. Third-party arrangements like these offer the opportunity for directed lending efforts that an institution could not achieve by relying only on a branch network delivery system. Institutions seeking to increase loan production with low- and moderate-income and minority borrowers should also consider purchasing loan production from mortgage brokers whose loan customers include low- and moderate-income borrowers and African-American and Hispanic borrowers. Purchased loan production can have a positive impact on CRA performance and lenders should not overlook, as a fall-back position, the desirability of purchasing certain types of loan production to compensate for less stellar market share results in directly originated lending.

The public's role in the CRA examination process is strengthened by the revised CRA regulations. Each federal financial supervisory agency publishes a list at least 30 days in advance of the quarter for those institutions scheduled to undergo CRA examinations in the next calendar quarter. The publication of the examination schedule serves as a reminder to members of the public concerning the opportunity to submit comments to an institution's public CRA file regarding the CRA performance of any institution whose name appears on the list. If received prior to the start of an examination, these comments would be taken into consideration during the examination in addition to any comments already in the institution's public CRA file. Because the precise timing of any particular examination, cannot always be accurately judged, members of the public who seek to play a role in the CRA examination process should submit their comments as soon as possible after the examination list of institutions is published.

N O T E S

1. General Accounting Office Report GAO/GGD-96-23, *Community Reinvestment Act: Challenges Remain to Successfully Implement CRA,* November 1995, p. 26.
2. Id., pages 28 and 29.
3. "Ludwig Urges Diligence by Bankers in Implementing Fair-Lending Law," *American Banker* 159, no. 137 (July 19, 1994), p. 2.
4. Id.

CHAPTER 10

Procedures for Third-Party Comment on Applications

The public has played a key role in enforcing CRA in both the applications review and the CRA examination process. Applications filed by institutions for expansion are a matter of public record, and the regulators invite public comment when they are considering them. When CRA ratings became public, members of the public were provided with more information to use in deciding whether to protest an application or patronize an institution.

Third parties have the opportunity to comment on an applicant's CRA performance record during the application process. The CRA requires federal financial supervisory agencies to consider the institution's entire CRA record as an integral component of the analysis of the convenience and needs of the community when processing certain types of applications under federal statutes governing regulated financial institutions.

The CRA lobby notice and the published notice of pending applications encourage public participation in the evaluation of applications for deposit facilities. The notice of a pending application must be published in a newspaper of general circulation in the affected community.

In cases in which an institution proposes to open a new office, the affected communities include the institution's headquarters and where the new office will be opened. In cases where an institution proposes to relocate an existing office, the affected communities include the institution's headquarters, the place where the office is presently located, and the place where the office will be relocated. The notice must be published at least three times over appropriate intervals during a 30-day period and must include the institution's name, the nature of the application, and the places where the institution proposes to do business.

As a result of the Federal Deposit Insurance Corporation Improvement Act of 1991, which added new Section 42 to the Federal Deposit Insurance Act, no FDIC-insured depository institution may close any branch without first submitting a 90-day notice of the proposed closing to the appropriate federal banking agency. The notice must contain a detailed statement of the reasons for closing the branch, along with statistical or other information in support of such reasons for the closing. The proposed notice of closing must also be posted in the branch 30 days prior to closing and mailed to customers not later than 90 days prior to closing. The notice may be included with regular account statements or as a separate mailing. All FDIC-insured depositories must adopt policies for branch closings along the lines noted above.

Persons interested in commenting on an application have a limited period of time within which to file their comments. Public comments that raise issues of CRA compliance are treated as protests to an application. The agencies must examine the nature and veracity of the protest. A review of the existing cases with respect to applications for deposit facilities and the CRA protests received reveals that the most significant assessment factor considered by the agencies relates to an institution's performance in making credit available in the community.

According to the 1989 Statement of the Federal Financial Supervisory Agencies Regarding the Community Reinvestment Act, a favorable CRA examination from a federal financial supervisory agency is an important, and often controlling, factor in the consideration of an institution's CRA record. It is not conclusive evidence, however, in the face of significant and documented allegations from a third-party commenter. This is especially the case when the examination is not recent or the particular issue raised in the application proceeding was not addressed in the institution's examination. In these instances, an applicant must submit sufficient data upon which the reviewing agency may base a decision regarding the institution's record of serving the convenience and needs of the institution's community. An applicant must also respond to specific substantive issues raised by the commenters or the reviewing agency.

The federal financial supervisory agencies issued the joint policy statement in March 1989 because third parties, particularly certain community organization groups, frequently use the opportunity for public comment to allege deficiencies in an institution's CRA performance record. With respect to the applications process, the 1989 joint policy statement recognizes that third-party commenters often seek an extension of the comment period. In many instances, this extension of the comment period can represent an attempt to frustrate completion of the transaction which is the subject of the application.

For this reason, the policy statement provides that, in accordance with the rules of the agencies, extensions of time for public comment will be provided only upon a showing of good cause or as otherwise permitted by agency regulations. For example, a brief extension would be permitted where the application has not been promptly made available for inspection by the parties or where there has been inadequate public notice of the application. The agencies do not believe that extensions of time are appropriate solely when the commenter desires more time to conduct discussions with an applicant. An extension of the comment period will only be for a brief period and normally will not be appropriate if the extension would extend the application processing period beyond the time limits established in the relevant statute or agency rules. A commenter that fails to submit comments on an application until after the close of the comment period (or any extension) may be precluded from participation.

Parties desiring to comment on applications, including those wishing to comment on the CRA record of a particular financial institution, must do so promptly and within the time periods specified in the rules of the appropriate reviewing agency and the relevant public notices. The agencies believe that this is important in order for them to carry out their responsibility to process applications within applicable time limits consistent with the public interest.

In connection with the protests lodged by community organizations and others, agencies have often found private meetings between an applicant and a protestant to be helpful. Such meetings may clarify the matters at issue, assist the agencies in determining whether additional information is required, help to plan the direction of the necessary analysis, and, in some instances, resolve differences based on misunderstandings between the parties. These meetings often provide the protestant and applicant with an opportunity to submit information to clarify or to support points made in their written submissions.

Protests have played a major role in the applications process. The potential for a protest by community groups or other members of the public has provided community groups with a measure of leverage over institutions wishing to expand and has added an element to the process beyond the potential for application denial. Many bankers have complained that community groups have used protests of applications and the threat of adverse publicity, delay, possible public hearings—and their attendant costs—to force lending commitments from institutions attempting to expand.[1] In some cases, agreements have been reached between bankers and community groups and then protests have been withdrawn and applications approved. In other cases, the regulators have approved the application after evaluating the protests and determining that the application did not warrant a denial.

Table 10–1 shows the number of applications from 1989 to 1994 that had protests lodged against them and the number of protested applications that resulted in denials on CRA grounds.[2]

While Table 10–1 generally shows a marked increase in the number of applications subject to protest, the number of protested applications that resulted in denials on CRA grounds has not similarly increased. This fuels the belief of national community organization groups that regulatory approval of expansion applications is a foregone conclusion. Study of Table 10–1 shows that applications submitted to the FRB and the OCC have shown the most marked increase in the number of protested applications. This generally reflects the fact that institutions with applications on file with those two agencies are generally the largest financial institutions in the land (either

T A B L E   10–1

Number of Applications with CRA-Related Protests
and Denials, from 1989 through 1994

	FRB		FDIC	
Year	Protested	Denied	Protested	Denied
1989	16	1	7	0
1990	27	0	7	0
1991	24	1	4	0
1992	28	0	0	0
1993	58	1	16	0
1994	55	0	13	0

	OCC		OTS	
Year	Protested	Denied	Protested	Denied
1989	8	0	10	1
1990	6	0	7	0
1991	5	0	3	0
1992	9	1	7	0
1993	14	0	3	0
1994	28	0	5	0

national banks or bank holding companies) and therefore serve as a lightning rod to attract high-profile national community organizations seeking to extract the largest reinvestment commitment possible. As previously described in the second section of Chapter 2, since 1990, voluntary community reinvestment commitments have increased exponentially, leading to indirect credit allocation. The very success, however, of community activists in obtaining such large reinvestment commitments has led to protests on applications that effectively cancel each other out. For example, in Wells Fargo & Company's 1996 acquisition of First Interstate Bancorp, one group of community activists led by the Greenlining Institute, negotiated a 10-year $45 billion reinvestment commitment. That commitment deflated what had been significant opposition to the merger. In contrast, the California Reinvestment Committee, an advocacy group representing numerous small community organizations, sought to continue the protested application, but to no avail in light of the massive reinvestment commitment by Wells Fargo designed to preempt the activists' protest.

Protesting applications has become almost a cottage industry. Consider that approximately 135 commenters supported or commented favorably about the CRA performance record of Wells Fargo. More than 600 commenters either opposed Wells Fargo's expansion application, requested that the FRB approve the merger subject to conditions suggested by the commenter, or expressed concerns about the CRA performance record of Wells Fargo or First Interstate.

A similar split developed in 1995 when Chemical Banking Corporation bid for Chase Manhattan Corporation, although with different results. The more prominent community activist groups fought for large reinvestment commitments. Chemical Banking Corporation, however, countered the demand by agreeing to continue funding for scores of local community programs Chemical was already supporting. These smaller groups then agreed to testify on Chemical's behalf, blunting the effect of national protests. In high-profile acquisition expansion proposals, the number of protests to the application is such that almost inevitably some community activist will be on the side of the acquiring bank, thus rendering less potent all protests filed by community activists against the expansion proposal.

Although the agencies believe that ongoing discussion between a financial institution and members of the institution's community is the best way to determine a community's needs, any decision to negotiate or to reach a formal agreement, either during or outside of the applications process, is at the discretion of the parties. The agencies may, in appropriate cases, facilitate private meetings and may have their representatives attend them. In doing so, however, the agencies will maintain a neutral role. Attendance and participation by the parties is voluntary. The purpose of such private meetings is not to provide a forum for the negotiation of a formal agreement among the parties. The agencies will not require or enforce such agreements. Moreover, the agencies do not believe that it is appropriate to suspend the processing of an application to allow the parties to conclude negotiations or to reach a settlement unless requested by the applicant.

The agencies will act on an application once they have obtained a record sufficient to support a determination in the matter.

Each agency may, under certain circumstances, order a public meeting, hearing, or oral argument. For example, an agency may find that a public meeting or hearing on an application would be helpful in order to develop a complete record for decision. A public meeting or hearing may be ordered if the written submissions and materials presented at the private meetings do not develop an application record that the reviewing agency believes is sufficient for making a decision. In such situations, the decision to call a public meeting or hearing would not be based solely on the inability of the parties to reconcile their differences in private meetings, but rather on the need of the reviewing agency for additional information that might be collected through such a process. Each agency follows its own regulations and procedures with respect to ordering public meetings, hearings, or oral arguments.

Community groups and some members of Congress have described the applications approval process as not being an effective enforcement mechanism for CRA because the regulators do not always deny applications on the basis of an applicant's poor CRA performance. Table 10–2, extracted from a 1995 General Accounting Office report to Congress, shows the number of applications denied on the basis of poor CRA performance since 1989.[3]

The FRB and FDIC have approved applications with commitments.[4] An example might include increased lending efforts in targeted neighborhoods. In the view of these two agencies, approval of applications with commitments provides the regulators with better enforcement leverage by explicitly tying an application's approval to tangible improvement of the applicant's CRA performance.[5] However, regulatory guidance states that commitments can only remedy specific problems in an otherwise satisfactory CRA record and cannot be the basis for the approval of an application.

The OCC and OTS do not typically approve applications with commitments but instead prefer to approve applications conditionally, if deemed appropriate.[6] The conditions for such approvals may be similar to commitments; however, the applicant institution must meet the conditions before consummation of the

T A B L E 10–2

Applications and CRA-Related Denials by the
Regulators from 1989 through 1994

	FRB		FDIC	
Year	Applications	Denials	Applications	Denials
1989	761	1	2,056	0
1990	696	0	2,099	0
1991	551	1	1,839	0
1992	619	0	1,891	0
1993	821	2	2,181	0
1994	826	0	2,883	3
	OCC		OTS	
Year	Applications	Denials	Applications	Denials
1989	2,782	2	939	1
1990	3,149	2	893	0
1991	2,630	0	573	0
1992	2,610	4	837	0
1993	3,612	0	785	0
1994	4,368	0	1,010	0

transaction for which it has applied.[7] An example of a condition
might be to require an applicant with a "needs to improve" CRA
rating that is seeking to open a branch office to upgrade the institution's rating to "satisfactory" before opening the branch.[8] Table
10–3 shows the number of applications approved with commitments since 1989 by the FRB and FDIC and shows the number of
applications approved with conditions by the OCC and OTS.[9]

Institutions considering expansion plans are aware of the
role CRA plays in the approval process. A dearth of applications
from institutions with adverse CRA evaluations is at best equiv-
ocal on the issue of commitment to CRA compliance. Institutions declining expansion opportunities due to CRA considerations do so not to avoid CRA compliance, but rather in
recognition of the fact that CRA compliance must be improved
before the application can be submitted with any hope of
approval.

T A B L E 10–3

Number of Applications Approved with CRA-Related Commitments or Conditions from 1989 through 1994

Year	FRB Approved with Commitments	FDIC Approved with Commitments	OCC Approved with Conditions	OTS Approved with Conditions
1989	5	0	15	2
1990	6	0	26	1
1991	7	0	18	1
1992	4	0	20	0
1993	9	0	18	0
1994	22	1	11	1

The opportunity for third-party comment concerning an applicant institution's CRA performance record can present a procedural maze, delayed processing, additional cost, and perhaps even frustration of the transaction which is the subject of the application. An institution contemplating expansion should make sure that the institution's CRA performance is at least satisfactory or reconsider submitting an application. Most institutions would prefer avoiding the adverse publicity and needless expense of filing an application only to be denied. If an institution perceives that its application for expansion is likely to be denied, the institution may choose to withdraw the application rather than have the application formally denied. Given that CRA compliance is a mandatory obligation which confronts virtually all bank and thrift institutions, institutions are well-advised to make CRA compliance a part of their routine management and operational structure, since the failure to comply with the CRA will almost certainly adversely affect the institution when the institution requires regulatory approval on an application at a later date.

Aside from the unfavorable impact that an unsatisfactory CRA performance record may have on an institution's applications process, members of the Federal Home Loan Bank System (which mainly include the nation's thrifts and the now majority of nonthrift members such as commercial banks) can lose access to long-term Federal Home Loan Bank (FHLB) advances as a result of a deficient CRA record. In March 1992, the Federal Housing Finance Board (FHFB) began its first review of the "Community Support Statements" that must be filed by the more than 5,000 institutions that are members of the FHLBs. The Community Support Statements, which outline minority and low-income lending goals and programs, rest heavily on CRA compliance.

In April 1992, Avondale Federal Savings Bank (Avondale), a member of the FHLB of Chicago, was the subject of a complaint filed by the Association of Community Organizations for Reform Now (ACORN). The complaint filed by ACORN was filed under the "Community Support Requirements" of the FHFB regulations. The ACORN complaint noted that Avondale rejected African-Americans and Hispanic applicants three times as often as whites. Thrifts like Avondale and other FHLB members that are challenged by community groups are brought up for review before the FHFB, which oversees the FHLBs. Should an FHLB member fail its community reinvestment review, the FHFB can then force the institution to install a reinvestment action plan, which is evaluated after one year by the FHFB. Failure to comply with the community reinvestment plan can trigger a number of disciplinary actions, the harshest of which is cutting off access to long-term FHLB advances. Such a move could severely penalize, if not cripple, some thrifts that depend on the FHLB's below-market-rate loans to fund their operations.

NOTES

1. General Accounting Office GAO/GGD-96-23, *Community Reinvestment Act: Challenges Remain to Successfully Implement CRA,* November 1995, p. 31.
2. Id., p. 32.
3. Id., p. 30.
4. Id.
5. Id.
6. Id.
7. Id.
8. Id.
9. Id., p. 31.

CHAPTER 11

Administrative Enforcement

CRA is enforced by the federal financial supervisory agency having general regulatory authority over a financial institution. The OCC supervises national banks. The FRB supervises (1) state banks that are members of the Federal Reserve System, and (2) bank holding companies. The FDIC supervises state-chartered commercial banks and savings banks that are not members of the Federal Reserve System but whose deposits are insured by the FDIC. The OTS supervises (1) savings associations whose deposits are insured by the FDIC, and (2) savings and loan holding companies.

Because credit unions and other depositary institutions are not within the definition of regulated financial institutions, the federal financial supervisory agencies having jurisdiction over those institutions are not given any enforcement responsibilities under the CRA.

No federal financial supervisory agency has primary responsibility for enforcement of the CRA. Concern over a lack of consistency in enforcement of the CRA prompted the federal financial supervisory agencies to issue joint regulations with respect to implementation of the substantive provisions of the CRA.

The supervisory agencies are required to consider an institution's record of meeting its entire community's credit needs, including low- and moderate-income neighborhoods, as part of the overall examination process. A large measure of discretion is afforded the agencies with respect to the emphasis placed on an institution's CRA record and the determination of an entire community's credit needs.

Upon the completion of each examination of an institution, the examining agency is required to prepare a written evaluation of the institution's CRA compliance record. This written evaluation includes the institution's record of meeting the credit needs of the institution's entire community, particularly low- and moderate-income neighborhoods.

The public has played a key role in enforcing CRA in both the applications review and the CRA examination process. This role was strengthened by amendments to CRA enacted in 1989 and in 1991. Applications filed by institutions for expansion are a matter of public record, and the regulators invite public comment when they are considering them. When CRA ratings became public, members of the public were provided with more information to use in deciding whether to protest an application or patronize an institution.

Examination and enforcement of the CRA have varied considerably among the federal financial supervisory agencies. In addition to their responsibilities for examining institutions for CRA performance, the federal financial supervisory agencies have been, since the late 1960s, responsible for examining and enforcing laws and regulations related to various consumer protection or civil rights laws and regulations. These laws include CRA, and the supervisory agencies monitor compliance with them through compliance examinations.

Since the late 1960s, the number of laws and regulations covered by compliance examinations has increased to over 20. Believing that bank operations had become too complex to be adequately covered by a single group of examiners, the FRB was the first federal financial supervisory agency to establish a special compliance examiner program in 1977, responsible for performing compliance examinations separately from safety and soundness examinations.[1]

The FDIC initiated a compliance examiner program in the late 1970s that established a compliance specialty but did not represent a separate career path and did not preclude examiners from also conducting safety and soundness examinations.[2] According to a seminal 1995 General Accounting Office report to Congress, the FDIC did not establish an entirely separate compliance examiner force exclusively responsible for compliance examinations until 1990, and the FDIC's compliance examiner program was not fully staffed until the end of 1993.[3] The compliance examiners remained part of the FDIC's Division of Supervision until an August 1994 reorganization that consolidated activities formerly divided between the Division of Supervision and the Office of Consumer Affairs into a single Division of Compliance and Consumer Affairs.

The OCC established a compliance examination specialty in the late 1970s.[4] According to the GAO report, the specialty did not represent a separate career path for examiners and often resulted in examiners spending only a portion of their time doing compliance examinations, with junior examiners usually responsible for doing compliance examinations.[5] The OCC began to develop a separate compliance program with a separate compliance examiner career path in 1993.[6]

Although the OTS supervises savings associations, as opposed to banks, the OTS is responsible for assessing compliance with the same compliance laws and regulations as the federal bank regulatory agencies. In 1989, the OTS established a separate compliance examiner program in which compliance examinations are conducted by specially trained, career professional staffs in the OTS regional offices.[7]

Table 11–1 shows the number of institutions subject to examination and the number of compliance examiners for each regulator at year-end for the period beginning in 1988.[8]

Review of Table 11–1 should be instructive for an institution to determine how thinly stretched the specialized compliance examination staff might be at a particular federal financial supervisory agency. Clearly the FRB, with examiner staffing levels running at levels approximately four times greater than the other three federal financial supervisory agencies, enjoys luxuries that the other supervisory agencies do not have. For that reason, state member banks regulated by the FRB generally receive compliance examinations far more frequently than

T A B L E   11–1

Number of Banks, Thrifts, and Compliance Examiners
per Regulator from Year-End 1988 to Year-End 1994

	FRB		FDIC	
Year	Banks	Examiners	Banks	Examiners
1988	1,063	116	8,207	22
1989	1,047	124	7,957	22
1990	1,014	137	7,838	22
1991	982	164	7,630	89
1992	957	201	7,431	151
1993	968	198	7,206	265
1994	979	246	7,031	300

	OCC		OTS	
Year	Banks	Examiners	Thrifts	Examiners
1988	4,435	N/A	2,970	N/A
1989	4,170	N/A	2,898	N/A
1990	3,973	N/A	2,541	N/A
1991	3,801	N/A	2,208	82
1992	3,598	N/A	1,954	92
1993	3,321	94	1,730	105
1994	3,078	170	1,543	105

Note: Where a regulator did not maintain a separate compliance examiner program or was unable to provide
data, it is noted in the table by an "N/A." For example, the OTS was unable to provide the number of
compliance examiners before 1991.

do national banks, OTS-regulated thrifts, or FDIC-regulated
nonmember banks. In addition, anecdotal evidence suggests
that continued shrinkage in the thrift industry and related
staffing cuts at the OTS have reduced that agency's specialized
compliance examination staff beyond the levels of 1994. Given
continued questions about the viability of the OTS relative to
the shrinking number of institutions that the agency regulates,
OTS-regulated thrifts may receive more uneven CRA performance evaluations under the revised CRA regulations than will
institutions regulated by the FRB, the FDIC, or the OCC.

A compliance examination generally results in two ratings:
(1) a compliance rating for an institution's overall compliance

effort with regard to various laws, other than CRA, covered by the compliance examination and (2) a CRA rating for the institution's compliance with CRA. Although the federal financial supervisory agencies may perform a CRA examination separately from a compliance examination, the seminal 1995 GAO report indicated the federal financial supervisory agencies performed CRA examinations together with compliance examinations.[9]

Although there have been fluctuations over time, approximately 90 percent of all institutions examined for CRA compliance have received a "satisfactory" rating or better since July 1990 when, as a result of amendments to CRA, ratings were made public, and the rating scale was changed.[10] Table 9–1 shows aggregate CRA ratings and ratings for each federal financial supervisory agency since July 1, 1990, when the regulators began publicly disclosing CRA ratings. As previously noted, the traditional bell curve of CRA compliance is likely to change over time under the revised CRA regulations, for it is not likely that federal financial supervisory agencies undertook more than two years of painstaking rulemaking procedures in order that 90 percent of the class will continue to receive a rating of satisfactory or better. Institutions that are most vulnerable to receiving a CRA performance evaluation of "needs to improve" or worse are those that (1) have a disproportionately small share of the low- and moderate-income lending market relative to the institutions' overall market shares, and (2) have not undertaken a concerted effort to identify low- and moderate-income credit opportunities or those markets.

The only enforcement mechanism provided in the CRA is the power to deny an application for failure to carry out the responsibilities imposed under the act. It is not uncommon, however, for a supervisory agency's approval of an application to be granted conditionally. See Chapter 10. This conditional approval is subject to the assurance by the institution to fulfill certain commitments.

In a 1994 legal opinion, the U.S. Justice Department Office of Legal Counsel opined that the federal financial supervisory agencies are not authorized to bring cease-and-desist and other corrective actions under Section 8 of the Federal Deposit Insurance Act to enforce the CRA. The conclusion of the Justice Department was

based on the rationale (1) that the CRA application evaluation
and approval procedure is the exclusive enforcement mechanism
authorized by Congress; and (2) that enforcement under Section 8
of the Federal Deposit Insurance Act is unavailable because the
CRA does not impose an obligation that could provide the basis for
an agency cease-and-desist order.[11] Furthermore, a failure to comply with the substantive requirements of the CRA or its implementing regulations may also involve a violation of the nondis-
crimination statutes, which may provide their own sanctions.
Widespread, repeat/uncorrected, or otherwise substantive violations of antidiscrimination laws and regulations are significant
adverse factors in an institution's CRA performance record, and
such fair lending violations will prompt enforcement actions
under the Equal Credit Opportunity Act (ECOA), Fair Housing
Act (FHA), or other applicable fair lending rules.

Prior to the issuance of the Justice Department's legal
opinion that regulators lacked authority to use any enforcement
mechanism for CRA compliance other than measures taken in
the context of an application, only a few enforcement actions
had been taken to address CRA violations. According to a seminal 1995 GAO report, enforcement actions taken to date have
only been with the consent of the affected institutions. Kenneth
Thomas, who wrote a 1993 ground-breaking work on CRA public performance evaluations, reports that the first cease-and-
desist order issued largely on CRA grounds was issued in
February 1991 against Mercantile Savings Bank, a now defunct
Mississippi savings association.[12] The picture that emerges from
the GAO report is that regulators have used enforcement
actions to address CRA deficiencies as one of many areas of
technical consumer law compliance violations.

Private individuals have been unable to establish a cause
of action under the CRA. In *Harambee Uhuru School Inc. v.
Kemp*,[13] the court held that the CRA does not imply a private
right of action against banks for refusing to make loans to low-
and moderate-income applicants. A nonprofit preschool successfully solicited loans from community block grant funds and private sources to purchase property for the school's use and later
obtained a loan and a rehabilitation grant from city authorities.
The nonprofit preschool later needed more funds, but a bank

refused to extend credit, a decision the school claimed was racially motivated. The school sued the bank under the CRA, but the court held that the statute does not authorize a private individual to file suit or pursue other remedies for violation of any of the statute's provisions.

While the CRA does not invest in any individual a particular right or the power to seek redress therefor, the ECOA and FHA, in contrast, create standing in individuals to seek redress for violations of those acts, which acts address transactions between financial institutions and individuals. Many individuals have successfully enforced their rights established by those fair lending acts. If the CRA can be interpreted to allow agency enforcement actions, it could also be interpreted to create an implied private right of action to enforce the CRA. Protection of individual rights is the essence of the judicial, as opposed to legislative, function. The CRA, on the other hand, does not purport to create any individual rights. Instead, the CRA's goal is to encourage neighborhood revitalization. The judicial function, that is, the enforcement function, has no place under the CRA.

Had Congress wished to allow enforcement actions under the CRA, it would have done so in clear fashion. Instead, Congress has established a comprehensive framework to combat discrimination, including redlining and disinvestment, employing a number of tools. Taken together, the CRA, HMDA, ECOA, and FHA establish a multifaceted, integrated approach to combatting discrimination through, among other things, enforcement actions under the ECOA and FHA, reporting and public disclosures under HMDA and the CRA (informing market-driven compliance incentives), and through the supervision and regulation process whereby CRA issues figure into bank and thrift examinations and application processes.

NOTES

1. General Accounting Office Report GAO/GGD-96-23, *Community Reinvestment Act: Challenges Remain to Successfully Implement CRA,* November 1995, p. 20.
2. Id.
3. Id.

4. Id., p. 21.

5. Id.

6. Id.

7. Id.

8. Id.

9. Id., p. 26.

10. Id.

11. Memorandum for Eugene A. Ludwig, Comptroller of the Currency, from Walter Dellinger, Assistant Attorney General, U.S. Department of Justice Office of Legal Counsel (December 15, 1994).

12. Kenneth H. Thomas, *Community Reinvestment Performance: Making CRA Work for Banks, Communities and Regulators* (1993). Probus Publishing Company, Chicago, Illinois.

13. No. C2-90-949 (S.D. Ohio, Sept. 30, 1992).

CHAPTER 12

A Global View on What Revised CRA Enforcement Means to the Banking Industry

A trend visible on the horizon in mid-1996 may foreshadow the greatest effect of the revised CRA regulatory assessment process. A rising delinquency level for loans originated pursuant to nontraditional lending programs highlights the relationship between community reinvestment activities and safe and sound banking practices. As the American economy has moved from a credit contraction cycle in the late 1980s and early 1990s to the mid-1990s' booming stock market and flush economy, the revised CRA assessment process may well contribute to the next cycle of credit losses. When the Treasury Department's full faith and credit guarantee of the FDIC deposit insurance funds is put at risk (and the taxpayers' commitment becomes plainly visible), the effects of the revised CRA regulatory assessment process will be considered in a far different light than the revised process was considered at the time of its inception. The effects of the revised CRA regulatory assessment process will over the coming decade prompt numerous academic studies, economic research reports, and congressional hearings and reports, but some of the most important anticipated effects are noted in this chapter.

The revised process by which CRA performance evaluations are conducted represents an ever-escalating cost of compliance and continues to serve as a competitive disadvantage relative to other competing firms not subject to CRA compliance and the extensive regulation to which FDIC-insured lending institutions are subject, although both such regulated and non-regulated institutions increasingly compete for the same business. Moreover, the revised regulatory assessment process does not eliminate subjective judgment on the part of examiners, such that the rules' standards will continue to be applied inconsistently from one institution to the next, resulting in competitive disadvantage and other adverse effects. The revised CRA assessment process contributes to a de facto safe harbor in the applications process for superregional and other money center banks that have the resources to enter into significant CRA lending commitments. The competitive frenzy to attain favorable market share in lending to low- and moderate-income borrowers will ultimately lead to higher foreclosure rates.

The revised regulations represent an increase in the regulatory burden imposed on financial institutions, except for small institutions under the $250 million asset threshold. It is not at all clear that the additional burdens represented by the revised CRA regulations will produce any incremental gain in credit availability to creditworthy persons because both financial institutions and federal financial supervisory agencies have invested such tremendous compliance efforts in meeting the letter and spirit of the fair lending laws—availability of credit to all creditworthy persons in the marketplace. Query how any gain in credit availability to creditworthy persons can be reliably measured as a consequence of the revised CRA evaluation process.

The revised CRA regulations continue to allow the exercise of subjective judgment on the part of the examiners. The evidence of inconsistency in CRA performance ratings revealed from the groundbreaking 1995 GAO report to Congress on CRA, as chronicled in Chapter 9, and the performance evaluations conducted through the first four months of 1996 reveal that inconsistency of application from one institution to the next continues under the revised CRA regulations in a fashion similar to that identified in the GAO report. This results in competitive disadvantage. At minimum, OTS-regulated thrifts would appear to be most disadvantaged and banking institutions regulated by the FRB are most advantaged by the inconsistency in application of CRA performance ratings across the industry.

With market share analysis likely to be regarded as one of the most probative indicators of CRA performance under the lending test, institutions that are currently market leaders in low- and moderate-income neighborhoods are rewarded. The new rating system will reinforce the dominance of the current market leader in low- and moderate-income neighborhoods and enable improvement in its market shares elsewhere by reason of (1) the favorable public relations associated with leadership in CRA lending and (2) by reason of the vastly improved posture that an institution's CRA rating would give the institution for purposes of making acquisitions or otherwise seeking expansion of the institution's activities through the application process.

A de facto safe harbor has come to exist for those institutions that have the resources to enter into significant CRA lending commitments, as many of the large money center and super-regional banking organizations already have. It is not uncommon, and it is very probably the general rule, that the CRA lending commitments are made in exchange for the promise not to assert a CRA protest (although May 1996 trade press stories indicate that one prominent community activist group based in New York no longer subscribes to that formula).

The City of Cleveland pioneered the use of CRA protests by a municipality to extract favorable lending commitments from banks with a presence in that marketplace. The City of Cleveland has signed a number of reinvestment agreements with superregional banking organizations in which a particular superregional banking organization agrees to lend millions of dollars to consumers in disadvantaged neighborhoods and over a number of years. Banc One Corporation had generally not entered into reinvestment commitments but changed its tack after Banc One's acquisition application to acquire Valley National in 1992 was protested by the City of Cleveland. Banc One entered into an agreement with the City of Cleveland. Although not stated in that agreement, one can only imagine the City of Cleveland agreed not to protest Banc One's applications under the CRA.

The ability of large institutions to purchase what amounts to a safe harbor in this fashion, while being of tremendous benefit to the beneficiaries of the lending commitments and the communities in which they live, illustrates yet another competitive disadvantage for smaller institutions.

At the time this book goes to press, the trend for superregional banking organizations to enter into significant CRA lending commitments and other forms of revolutionary lending programs continues. For example, in fall 1995, NationsBank Corporation (NationsBank) announced that it would establish a five-year $500 million program for low-income borrowers with no down payment, no closing costs, and no application fees. In spring 1996, First Union Corporation announced a similar no-down-payment, no-closing-costs lending program for low-income borrowers. On a different front, the *CRA Bulletin,* a monthly newsletter published by Warren, Gorham & Lamont, reported that relaxed underwriting standards, higher loan-to-value ratios, and higher interest rates have increased foreclosure rates on loans originated in late 1994 and 1995.[1] According to a study of 20 million mortgage loans originated nationwide conducted by the Mortgage Research Group, a Jersey City, New Jersey–based research group, .012 percent of the loans originated went into foreclosure within seven months as contrasted to the three years it took for foreclosure rates to attain that level on loans originated in 1992.[2]

While there may be valid economic reasons which explain the rising delinquency trend, this report may foreshadow a trend in rising delinquencies on loans originated pursuant to *very* nontraditional lending programs.

An article appearing in the July 1996 *Federal Reserve Bulletin* considered the credit risk of loans extended pursuant to affordable home loan programs.[3] Entitled "Credit Risk, Credit Scoring and the Performance of Home Mortgages," the article analyzed the experience of secondary market institutions, private mortgage insurance ("PMI") companies and other portfolio lenders with affordable home loan programs intended to benefit low- and moderate-income and minority households and neighborhoods. For CRA-inspired loans (1) purchased by the secondary market or (2) insured by PMI companies, the article reports that delinquency rates have become the prime indicator of possibly unacceptable credit risk for loans extended under affordable home loan programs.[4] For example, Freddie Mac reports that the 60-day delinquency rate on loans purchased under its affordable home loan initiatives has been higher than on a peer group of traditionally underwritten mortgages.[5]

Because of the important role played by private mortgage insurance as an often necessary predicate to affordable home lending programs offered by lenders, study of the experience of PMI companies is also instructive in considering the performance of affordable home loan programs. The article reported on the experience of Mortgage Guaranty Insurance Corporation (MGIC), GE Capital Mortgage Insurance Corporation (GEMICO) and United Guaranty Corporation. The mortgage insurance companies reported that the delinquency rate on loans insured by them extended pursuant to affordable home lending programs was higher than the delinquency rate on the other loans such mortgage loan companies insure.[6] Of particular note, MGIC reported that borrowers who covered a 3 percent down payment themselves and had a third party provide an additional 2 percent (so-called 3/2 option loans) had a delinquency rate twice as high as borrowers who provided the entire 5% down payment.[7] According to the article, the experience of the PMI companies and the secondary market is too preliminary to determine whether the elevated delinquency rates on loans originated under affordable home lending programs will ultimately result in higher claim rates for PMI-insured loans and higher losses to portfolio lenders and the secondary market agencies.[8]

As these early tell-tale signs of undue risk appear, affordable lending programs are unlikely to be modified to eliminate or mitigate those innovative aspects of affordable lending initiatives which present undue credit risk.

Although difficult to imagine in 1996, these nontraditional lending standards will be looked at with a different eye when the country experiences its next adverse credit cycle. As of June 1996, the banking industry is and has been flush with profits during the last several years. When the country last experienced a terribly adverse credit cycle in the late 1980s, congressional hearings were held to focus on safety and soundness issues. How quickly society forgets that some of the maneuverings of the

1988 presidential election and late-1980 congressional hearings pertained to efforts to induce banking regulators to be more reasonable. Then OCC Comptroller Clarke was described as the "regulator from hell" in trade press stories for his firm and vigorous handling of safety and soundness issues. When the next cycle of credit losses occurs, as history suggests it inevitably must, the relaxed underwriting standards and unprecedented loan-to-value ratios introduced in the 1990s may well be rolled back as an aberration of a different time.

N O T E S

1. *CRA Bulletin* 5, no. 8 (May 1996).
2. Id.
3. *Federal Reserve Bulletin,*Volume 82 (July 1996), pp. 621–648.
4. Id.
5. Id., p. 642, quoting from comments made by Freddie Mac President Leland Brendsel in a July 21, 1995 *American Banker* article entitled "Freddie Sounds a Delinquency Alarm on Popular Lower-Income Mortgage."
6. *Federal Reserve Bulletin,* Volume 82 (July 1996), pp. 621–648.
7. Id., p. 644.
8. *Federal Reserve Bulletin,* Volume 82 (July 1996), pp. 621–648.

APPENDIX 1

Sample Format for Loan Distribution Analysis*

Metropolitan Statistical Area (MSA)		1993				1994			
		Total Applications	Approved #/%	Other #/%	Denied #/%	Total Applications	Approved #/%	Other** #/%	Denied #/%
Akron MSA (As of September 1995, 19 office locations, 3 located in low- and moderate-income tracts, 11 located in middle-income census tracts, 5 located in upper-income tracts, and 1 located in a minority tract)	Low- and moderate-income tracts	148	113 76.4%	4 2.7%	31 20.9%	302	200 66.2%	12 4.0%	90 29.8%
	Low- and moderate-income applicants	430	356 82.8%	21 4.9%	53 12.3%	615	422 68.6%	34 5.5%	159 25.9%
	Middle- and upper-income tracts	2,375	2,059 86.7%	76 3.2%	240 10.1%	2,827	2,331 82.5%	123 4.4%	373 13.2%
	Middle- and upper-income applicants	2,065	1,790 86.7%	58 2.8%	217 10.5%	2,501	2,097 83.8%	100 4.0%	304 12.2%
	Minority tracts	31	26 83.9%	0	5 16.1%	92	54 58.7%	4 4.3%	34 37.0%
	Minority applicants	107	89 83.2%	2 1.9%	16 15.0%	198	124 62.6%	7 3.5%	67 33.8%
	Joint minority and nonminority applicants	42	35 83.3%	1 2.4%	6 14.3%	68	53 77.9%	5 7.4%	7 10.14%

*Note: This sample only relates to HMDA loan applications. Similar analysis should be done for other types of loans such as consumer and commercial loan products.

**"Other" includes applications withdrawn, applications approved but not accepted, and applications whose incomplete files had been closed.

Sample Public File Comment Letter

Mr. Able CEO
President
ABC Savings Bank
1111 Road
Hometown, Your State

RE: CRA Public File Comment Letter

Dear Mr. CEO:

I am writing to thank you for inviting me to sponsor a table at the ABC Savings Bank First-Time Homebuyer Seminar held on Wednesday, April 16, 1996. Our company was flattered to be invited and even more proud to be present.

While all lenders are in business to make residential mortgage loans and many pay lip service to the first-time homebuyer market, I must commend ABC Savings Bank on the thoroughness of the presentations made by various bank officers on the different aspects of the mortgage lending process. I think management's willingness to meet the public in a forum such as this evidences management's desire to meet the community's credit needs. As one involved in the process of selling homes to many first-time homebuyers, the patience and thoroughness of bank management in responding to questions from the floor at the first-time homebuyer seminar was wonderful. The public and the lending community would be better served if more lenders were willing like ABC Savings Bank to come into the trenches, as it were, and conduct a seminar on first-time home buying opportunities.

Continued.

Concluded.

While the seminar was great, one possible suggestion for improvement at the next such seminar would be the following:
[To be completed by realtor]

Again I write to thank you for inviting our firm to participate in ABC Savings Bank's seminar on first-time homebuyers. I think you did the community a great service by sponsoring this seminar and bringing such credible speakers as Congressman Liberal Democrat to appear as a presenter at this seminar. So that the government banking agencies are aware of ABC Savings Bank's outstanding effort at meeting the community's credit needs, please place this letter in ABC Savings Bank's CRA public file of comment letters.

Sincerely yours,

John Realtor
President
All People's Realtor Company

INDEX

ACORN (Association of Community Organizations for Reform Now), 128
Advertising, 46, 47
Affordable housing programs, 22
   delinquency trends, 137
   foreclosure trends, 140
Application for a deposit facility
   approval
      conditionally, 125
      with comments, 125
   approval rates, 3
   comment period, 121
   de facto safe harbor, 138, 139
   defined, 2
   denial on basis of CRA performance, 3, 4, 122, 125, 133
   newspaper notice of pending application, 119
   protest, 120, 122
   withdrawal, 127
Assessment area, 17, 20, 31, 34, 35, 44, 63
   identification in public file, 79
   limited purpose book, 101
   wholesale book, 101
ATM, 31, 34, 58
Avondale Federal Savings Bank, 128

Banc One Corporation, 139
Bank Holding Company Act of 1956, 2, 9
Bank views on CRA, 13
Banking Act of 1935, 8
Bilingual staff, importance of, 59
Block numbering area, definition, 25
Board of Governors of the Federal Reserve System, 9, 11, 19, 69
   application approval with commitments, 125
   enforcement, 129
Branch, 22, 31, 34, 58
   branch siting decision, 59
   closure, 120
   identification in public file, 79
   limited purpose bank designation, 99
   wholesale bank designation, 99
Brownfields, 23

California Reinvestment Committee, 123
CDC (community development corporation), 23
CDFI (community development financial institution), 22, 54–55
CEBA bank, 30
Census Bureau (See United States Department of the Census)
Census tracts, 25
CFR
   (Part 25), 11, 19
   (Part 228), 11, 19
   (Part 345), 11, 19
   (Part 563(e)), 11, 19
Charitable giving, 57
Chase Manhattan Corporation, 124
Chemical Banking Corporation, 124
Chevy Chase Federal Savings Bank, 46, 59, 60
Clarke, Robert, 142
Cleveland, City of, 139
Clinton, President William J., 13
CMSA (consolidated metropolitan statistical area), 21, 32, 34, 39
Commitments, lending, 13, 18, 48
   de facto safe harbor to application protest, 138–139
   protested applications, 122, 124
Community development, 21
Community development loan, 2, 23, 52, 54, 69, 70, 101
Community development service, 23–25, 61
Community development test, 23, 97
Community Reinvestment Act
   applicability, 2
   compliance violations, 84
   convenience and needs criteria, 8, 10
   coverage, 1
   legislative history, 7–10
   public CRA evaluation, 9
   purpose, 1, 8
CRA Disclosure Statement, 50, 76
   inclusion in public file, 81
CRA Statement, 21, 84, 85

Other books of interest to you from Irwin Professional Publishing . . .

BANKING REDEFINED
How Super Regional Powerhouses Are Reshaping Financial Services
John Spiegel, Alan Gart, Steven Gart

The banking industry is redefining itself every day. The media is reporting
such mega deals as First Chicago and NBD, First Union and First Fidelity,
and Fleet, Shawmut and NatWest. The eyes of the industry are on the
SuperRegional banks. Not only are they some of banking's most competitive
and profitable institutions, they are prime movers in the renewed wave of
consolidation. *Banking Redefined* explores the major problems and challenges facing the banking industry and their impact on the bank franchise.
The ultimate success or failure of banks will rest on their ability to relate
meaningfully in the consuming public. This book addresses the obstacles,
and reasons behind why some banks succeeded and others succumbed.

450 pp.   ISBN: 0-7863-0959-8 $37.50 ©1996

COMMUNITY BANK SURVIVAL GUIDE
Overcoming the Challenges of an Increasingly
Competitive Marketplace
Douglas V. Austin

The Community Bank Survival Guide calls upon community banks to aban-
don "traditional" and look to the future—now—to impact the way each institution conducts its business—from the procedures and policies in place to
the equipment in use by the employees. This book describes techniques for
survival and devotes coverage to the importance of developing leadership in
the community bank and in the surrounding community. Changing the cul-
ture to one that is more sales and marketing driven—perhaps the most
important change necessary for survival—is covered in great detail.

150 pp.   ISBN: 0-7863-1107-X $19.95 ©1997

GUIDE TO NATIONAL BANKING LAW
Jonathan L. Levin

Driven by competitive forces, banks are under increasing pressure to tailor their products to the requirement of market niches and customer bases. However, the movement toward becoming customer-oriented has given the Office of the Controller of the Currency a reason to shift their examination process to a "supervision by risk" model. As a result, a greater emphasis is being placed on knowledge, understanding, and execution of national banking law. *The Guide To National Banking Law* is a complete catalogue and summary of all laws specifically governing the operations of national banks.

250 pp.   ISBN: 0-7863-1057-X $37.50 ©1996

HANDBOOK OF REAL ESTATE LENDING
Kathleen Sindell

The Handbook of Real Estate Lending covers the unique needs of real estate and mortgage lending highlighting the opportunities and the potential problems typically faced in the field. An excellent overview of the real estate side of the loan portfolio, this start-to-finish guide covers everything from basic background to hands-on strategies and procedures. This comprehensive review of real estate lending includes a thorough look at problem loans, from early warning signs to the aftermath of defaults. The guide contains key strategies for prevention and avoidance of potentially bad loans and the means to ensure protection from loss.

500 pp.   ISBN: 0-7863-0880-X $75.00 ©1996

SUPERCOMMUNITY BANKING STRATEGIES
Taking the Next Steps Toward Market Leadership
Anat Bird

In this continuation of the best-selling, *SuperCommunity Banking: A SuperStrategy for Success,* author Anat Bird returns with a new look at the institutions that have changed the banking industry. *SuperCommunity Banking Strategies* analyzes the challenges and opportunities facing community and SuperCommunity banks in this era of rapid technological change, consolidation, highly aggressive and often non-traditional competition.

400 pp.   ISBN: 0-7863-0996-2 $70.00 ©1996